SQL

The Ultimate Beginner's Guide for Becoming Fluent in SQL Programming

Mark Chen

Table of Content

3

Introduction

The SQL Language (short of System Query Language) has been pioneering the relational database industry ever since its conception during the 70s. Back then when hippy vans used to rule the streets, a company known as IDM dwelled deep into the concepts of creating a relational database theory (The DBMS) and a sub-language to accompany those systems. The language was first called SEQUEL! But later came to be known as SQL to avoid copyright issues.

In a world where digital information is the backbone of whole companies, the presence of relational databases has been as vital before as they are today. Certain organizations are always on the lookout for people who are able to properly maintain their whole database structures ensuring a safe and secured pipeline for information to be exchanged between/within companies and clients alike.

It is a common misconception that people who are responsible for these actions are some sort of digital deity with extraterrestrial abilities! Let us debunk this theory and tell you that SQL is a pretty straight forward language and with a little practice, anyone can pick it up! As long as you know English, you are good to go!

That is exactly the focus of this book. This book has been designed in such a way that the information conveyed are able to help programmers of all levels. Whether you are an absolute beginner with zero knowledge or moderately advanced one who might be looking for a brief reference guide, this book got you covered!

Throughout the book you will be introduced to the very roots of database systems, learn about the major components of SQL and discover the ways of creating and manipulating your own database while keeping it well protected and secured!

Learning SQL will not only give you an extremely versatile and powerful tool to retrieve data, it will also increase your weight in the job market by ten folds!

Don't waste any more time and jump right in! Your journey starts now....

Chapter One: Your First Step Into The World Of SQL

We realize that you must be very eager to directly jump into the world of SQL, but you should hold your heels for just a moment! Blindly running into the unknown is never a good thing and we have seen lots of people stumble going down that path. We are here to make sure you wouldn't make that mistake!

When a hunter first learns to hunt, he/she begins by first learning the very basics of the art of hunting. They train themselves in the art of holding a fishing pole before setting out in cold waters! Our methodology runs with a similar agenda; we believe that before letting you in on the vastness of SQL, you should first know a little bit about the very basics of the language. That is exactly what this chapter is going to be emphasizing on. So, let's begin our journey!

What Exactly Is SQL?

SQL is a programming language no doubt about that, but there is a very intricate difference which you should first understand when bringing this particular language in comparison with the other ones.

The most widely known language such as BASIC, C, C# or even Java are designed to be procedural languages. This simply means that whenever you want to solve a problem using these languages, it is utmost important that you write down the whole procedure or "Methods" following which the program will perform its job.

In case of SQL however, it is the exact opposite. SQL is not a procedural language and here, to solve a problem all you will have to do is tell SQL what needs to be done. Since SQL runs very closely interlinked with the relational database or (Database Management System), the database then takes over and calculates out the most efficient and quickest route into solving the problem.

The Glance At The SQL Statements

If you have ever created a program of even a single line, then you do know what a statement is. However, you don't need to start sweating now as we are not going to assume that you did! Statements are basically the specific words or sentences of two or three words in some cases, used to let the program know what you want it to do. When It comes to SQL command language (Fancy name for Statement), they have been divided into three categories:

- Data Defining Statements
- Data Manipulation Statements
- Data Handling Statements

We will be discussing all of these types in details throughout the book, but for now, have a look at the table below. This should give you a rough idea of the statements which are available at your disposable when working with SQL.

ADD	DEALLOCATE PREPARE	FREE LOCATOR
ALLOCATE CURSOR	DECLARE	GET DESCRIPTOR
ALLOCATE DESCRIPTOR	DECLARE LOCAL TEMPORARY TABLE	GET DIAGNOSTICS
ALTER DOMAIN	DELETE	GRANT PRIVILEGE
ALTER ROUTINE	DESCRIBE INPUT	GRANT ROLE

A Series of Reserved Words

In the programming world, the term "Reserved Words" generally holds a similar meaning when spanning across multiple languages. These are essentially a set of specific words and statements that are hard built inside the language framework (in this case SQL) which cannot be used at our own will to set up variable names. The list of statement above are all examples of Reserved words. Why should you keep this in mind? Just imagine the confusion when you might accidentally write something like the following!

ALTER SEQUENCE GENERATOR	DESCRIBE OUTPUT	HOLD LOCATOR
ALTER TABLE	DISCONNECT	INSERT
ALTER TRANSFORM	DROP	MERGE
ALTER TYPE	DROP ASSERTION	OPEN
CALL	DROP ATTRIBUTE	PREPARE
CLOSE	DROP CAST	RELEASE SAVEPOINT
COMMIT	DROP CHARACTER SET	RETURN
CONNECT	DROP COLLATION	REVOKE
CREATE	DROP COLUMN	ROLLBACK
CREATE ASSERTION	DROP CONSTRAINT	SAVEPOINT
CREATE CAST	DROP DEFAULT	SELECT
CREATE CHARACTER SET	DROP DOMAIN	SET CATALOG
CREATE COLLATION	DROP METHOD	SET CONNECTION
CREATE DOMAIN	DROP ORDERING	SET CONSTRAINTS
CREATE FUNCTION	DROP ROLE	SET DESCRIPTOR
CREATE METHOD	DROP ROUTINE	SET NAMES
CREATE ORDERING	DROP SCHEMA	SET PATH
CREATE PROCEDURE	DROP SCOPE	SET ROLE
CREATE ROLE	DROP SEQUENCE	SET SCHEMA

Something like that is definitely going to give your computer a very bad case of program headache!

The Different Types Of Data

A programming language is never static and throughout its course of evolution, it keeps on adding new features with added support for more data types. In case of SQL, it has a set of approximately 7 data types that have been initialized into the main frame.

- Numerics
- Binary
- Strings
- Booleans
- Datetimes
- Intervals
- XML

Each of these data types are the further divided into sub genres which we will be discussing shortly.

Numerics

Numerics are essentially the type of variables, or containers if you will, which hold numbers of different sizes and lengths. Numerics have been categorized into 5 different types:

- **INTEGER:** These are your typical whole numbers with no extended fractional part.
- **SMALLINT:** This is a data type similar to that of an integer, but differs just a bit in terms of precision implementation. The precision length of the data cannot be larger than that of the integer on the same

implementation. Meaning, if your integer's precision is 4, SMALLINT has to be either 4 or less.

- **BIGINT**: BIGINT works similarly like SMALLINT with the difference of the length being at least as big as the integer or greater than it.

- **NUMERIC**: These are data values which can hold a fractional component in conjunction to its integer counterpart.

- **DECIMAL**: The DECIMAL data type is similar to NUMERIC data type in terms of having a fractional part and precision. But the major difference here is that the length of your applied precision might be greater than the one which you have specified. If it is turns out to be greater, then by default the program will use the greater one.

- **REAL data type (Approximate Numeric)**: This data type will give you a single-precision floating-point number whose precision will be dependent on your SQP implementation, or more specifically on your hardware which can either be 32 bit 64 bit.

- **DOUBLE PRECISION data type (Approximate Numeric)**: This particular data type is a double-precision floating-point number whose precision also depends on the implementation. However, the word DOUBLE in itself also relies heavily on the implementation. The double precision is mostly used when several formats of scientific calculations are brought into the table.

- **FLOAT:** The benefit of using a float data type is that you are able to specify the level of precision. This is commonly used when a program is being developed with migration in mind in the sense that in the distant future, the current said program will be transferred to another hardware platform with different register sizes.

- **ARRAY Type:** The ARRAY type falls under the collection type and is not that much distinct in terms of CHARACTER and NUMERIC. But the prime difference here, is that instead of a single object, in an Array you will be able to hold multiple objects at once.

Strings

Strings or Character strings are also a set of data type which has been designed to hold long sentences of individual characters as well as manipulation of columns and rows. When talking about the characters first, they are sub-divided into three types:

- **CHARACTER data Type:** This data type will allow you to determine the number of characters a column or row will be able to hold. So, if you are using the syntax

CHAR (x), then you would be creating a column that can hold x number of characters.

- **CHARACTER VARYIN data type:** It is wise to use this type of data when you are going to be creating a column that has a varying number of characters. The syntax is VARCHAR (x) where x is the maximum number of characters permitted, if it is anything less than that, the row will adjust itself without leaving blank fields.

- **CHARACTER LARGE OBJECT data type:** This data type is primarily used to hold up large string characters that go beyond the boundaries of the CHARACTER data type.

Binary Strings

Introduced in SQL: 2008 the BINARY string data type are the fundamental understandable language of a digital computer. These have been yet again divided into three subclasses:

- **BINARY data type:** In this case, you will be able to define a column as BINARY where afterwards, the number of bytes you specify will determine the length of string the column will be able to hold. For example, a column of BINARY (15) will be able to hold a string of 16-byte length.

- **BINARY Varying data type:** This is used when you think that the length of the binary string might be variable. The syntax is VARBINARY (x) where x is the maximum length of the stored string.
- **BINARY LARGE OBJECT data type:** This is used for data that are made up of huge strings which exceeds the boundaries of BINARY type. Such strings include music files as well as graphical images.

Booleans

Boolean data types can hold only true or false value and nothing in between. This is useful when directing your program to a specific path as we will see in the coming chapters.

Datetime

The SQL library is comprised of about five different data type that are used when dealing with real time dates and times.

- **DATE data type:** The DATE data type is very simple and it is used to store the values of year, month and date in that particular order.
- **TIME WITHOUT TIME ZONE:** The TIME WITHOUT TIME ZONE stores only the hour, minute and second values of time.

- **TIMESTAMP WITHOUT TIME ZONE:** This one is much more versatile and includes the information for both date and time.

- **TIME WITH TIME ZONE data type:** This is pretty much the same as TIME WITHOUT TIME ZONE except for one difference. This data type holds the information of relating to the offset from the Universal Time in addition to the time values.

- **TIMESTAMP WITH TIME ZONE:** Similar to TIMESTAMP WITH TIME ZONE, this value just adds in the extra offset information from the Universal Time.

XML

Now this is a term with which you should be familiarized yourself with thoroughly because you will be dissecting this extensively in the future. The word XML is actually an acronym which stands for eXtensible Markup Language that simply defines a preliminary set of rules required to add mark ups to data. In simple words though, the usage of XML will enable you to share your data between various platforms.

The organization of data type is done using what are called "nodes".

The primary modifiers used for XML are SEQUENCE, CONTENT and DOCUMENT. While UNTYPED, ANY and XMLSCHEMA fall under the category of secondary modifiers.

Understanding SQL In A System Comprised Of Client/Server

What Is A Server?

The server is a fancy name given to the database server which is an integral part of a Client/ Server system and you will be interacting with this a lot. The main responsibility of the server is to hold the software of the server which is responsible for manipulating the commands that are received from the client and convert them into understandable commands for the database itself. The server also plays a great role when it comes to retrieving and sending the results of the actions performed by the said client.

What Is The Client?

The second part of the Client/Server system is the client which comprised of both a hardware and software component. In perspective, the computer of the client is referred to as the Hardware alongside the interface controlling the local area network. The feature that makes the clients distinctive is the software used.

The main purpose of the client is to display various information on the screen and simultaneously respond to them using any form of input device (keyboard, mouse etc.)

Alternatively, the clients have the opportunity allowing them to process input data from telecommunication links.

Chapter One: Concept Questions

Q1) SQL --?

a) Is a procedural language to solve problems

b) Runs with no link with the relational database

c) Requires you to write down different methods

d) Is not a procedural language that is used to solve problems

Answer: D

Q2) Which of the following is a SQL command language?

a) Data Defining Statement

b) Data Manipulating Statement

c) Data Handling Statements

d) All of the above

Answer: D

Q3) Which one of the following Is one of the 7 data types of SQL?

a) Integer

b) Booleans

c) Arrays

d) Float

Answer: B

Q4) Which one of the following is a Numeric?

a) SMALLINT

b) DATETIME

c) XML

d) BINARY

Answer: A

Q5) Which binary data type is used when you might have a huge binary strings?

a) BINARY LARGE OBJECT

b) BINARY Varying data type

c) BINARY data type

d) BINARY HUGE Datatype

Answer: A

Chapter Two: Know Your Relational Database

Now that you know a good deal about SQL, let me now talk about the mysterious "Database" about which I have been blabbering on and on up until this point of the book.

SO, What Are Databases?

The concept of a Database is pretty much trivial to say the least. Imagine that you have a heap load of files, each of them containing very crucial and important information. Naturally you would want to keep them safe right? So, probably you are going to store them inside a file cabinet or a re-enforced drawer to make sure that they are safe.

But we are no longer living in the old days and nowadays, everything is slowly becoming more and more digitized. Important documents and files are now stored in computer hard drives or even the cloud. These digital locations where the data are saved is referred to as computer "Databases".

Strictly speaking however, the term "Database" primarily refers to a collection of integrated records which consist of both data and metadata. The programming language "SQL" acts as a bridge between the user and the data base being used which data can be stored, edited or even manipulated as required.

You already know what is the meaning of data, metadata basically indicates formal structure following which the said data are being organized inside a database.

A Little Insight Into Database Size and Its Complexity

Different jobs and projects call for a different database size. Some might require extremely massive ones while others might require very simple smaller sized ones to store a few records. Regardless, all of the Database currently present can be categorized to fall under one of the three categories below:

- **A Personal Database:** This is designed with a very simple structure and holds a relatively small size. Recommended for a single person.
- **Departmental Database:** These databases are dedicated for a number of multiple users working together in an enclosed work group or a department. These bases are comparatively much more complex and are capable of handling the data of multiple users at the same time.
- **Enterprise Database:** These are basically the largest one which are made up of utmost complexity and allows the free flow of critical information of massive organizations.

It should be kept in mind that a good Database should have the following four criteria:

- The method through which data is stored should be easy and efficient.
- It should be reliable as to prevent data loss
- The method of data retrieval should also be quick and efficient
- There should be a good filtering system to ensure that all required data are found easily.

And how exactly is a database maintained?

The Database Management System

The answer to that question lies in the Database Management System or DBMS for short. The whole DBMS is pretty much a compilation of programs which are required to administer, define and ultimately process the databases including all of the interlinked applications. Alternatively, it can be said that the DBMS is a tool using which you will be able to create a suitable structure which will contain all of your data and provide you with easy accessibility.

```
SELECT SELECT FROM SELECT WHERE = WHERE
;
```

Flat Files: The Most Basic File Structure

Judging from the title of this chapter, you might think that Flat Files are simply a compilation of files squashed down under a hammer. But I assure you, that's not the case. Instead, flat file is pretty much a collection of data records following a specific format – particularly a list. The reason why I am calling it a "Simple Structure" is because it is void of any sort of metadata and it has a very minimalistic overhead.

Below is an example how you might create a list of names and addresses of your customers.

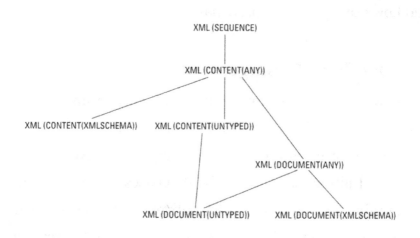

The Relational Database: The One That Sunk All The Other Models

And yes, the information in this section is worthy of its title. Relational Database did in fact blow out every other model before it out of the water. First established by Dr. Codd during the year of 1970, this particular model had a large difference which made the older models obsolete. The relation model did in fact allow you to change or modify any applications which were made throughout basing them on the older models. Fascinating right? So imagine a scenario where you are needed to add a column. You will be able to do that now without changing the procedures of the rest of the column in the table!

The Different Components Of A Relational Database

The flexibility here basically means that you are able to add, change or delete data without affecting in other tables. Which means, the table themselves are largely independent of each other. But what are these tables made up of? Here, we are going to have a look at exactly that!

Bear in mind that in terms of Databases, we are defining the Tables as a "Relation" or more specifically we are defining a two-dimensional array with rows and columns as a Relation. Each cell in an Array has the capacity to hold one value and there cannot be a duplicate row. Confused much? Let us give you an example relating to your favorite sports, The Baseball! Consider the statistics written on the back of a baseball card. The columns here contain his gaming statistics such his team, years, number of games played and so on while the row is covering those particular statistics throughout various years.

The way the whole table (relation) is organized is the structure and the written values are the data.

```
CREATE TABLE CUSTOMER (
CustID                    INTEGER
PRIMARY KEY,
LastName                  CHARACTER
VARYING (25),
FirstName                 CHARACTER
VARYING (20),
Address                   addr_typ,
Phone                     CHARACTER
VARYING (15)
) ;
```

Keep in mind that each column in this array is self-consistent. Which simply means that every column holds a similar meaning regardless of which row you are pointing at. As you can see, every column of our particular baseball player is holding a certain criteria or attribute of the player. Have a look at another example of a relation where customer data are being held.

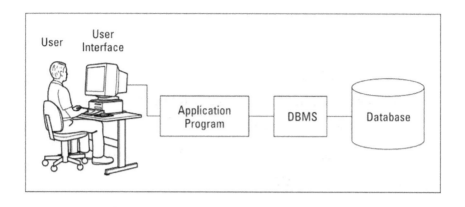

Introducing The "Views"

Standing on top of the Great Wall of China, a terrific view. But is that view this view? Not necessarily.

For this particular topic, I want you to go back to the point where I told you that a good database should contain the ability to filter data. The View is pretty much responsible for doing that. Imagine that your database has hundreds of table, but you are in need of only one column from Table 1 and another row from table 3. What are you going to do? Create a View of course!

Now, views are strictly a subset of the database which an application can process to eliminate all the data that are irrelevant to you requirements.

```
Harold Percival        26262 S. Howards
Mill Rd
Westminster CA92683
Jerry Appel            32323 S. River
```

Lane Rd

Santa

Ana   CA92705

Adrian Hansen   232 Glenwood Court

Anaheim   CA92640

John Baker   2222 Lafayette St

Garden Grov CA92643

Michael Pens   77730 S. New Era Rd

Irvine CA92715

Bob Michimoto   25252 S. Kelmsley Dr

Stanton   CA92610

Linda Smith   444 S.E. Seventh St

Costa

Mesa

CA92635

Robert Funnell   2424 Sheri Court

Anaheim   CA92640

Bill Checkal   9595 Curry Dr

Stanton   CA92610

Jed Style   3535 Randall St

Santa

Ana CA92705

Have a look at the sample view above. Here we have four tables. The Customer Table and the Invoice Table alongside two views: the Sales Manager's view and the Branch Manager's view. The Sales Manager's view consists of the all the information that falls under his required ones, namely – First Name, Last Name and Phone number. The Branch Manager's view however has already been specified a fixed limit only view the information within those particular columns.

Further Structural Organization: The Schemas, Domain and Constrains

You should understand that a database is not necessarily limited to having just a bunch of tables. There might be some additional underlying structures working at several different levels.

- **Schemas:** This is sometimes known as the Conceptual view which basically is the structure of the whole database. Alternatively, you can consider Schema as being the Metadata.
- **Domain:** These are specific attributes present in a relation. Or more specifically, these are specific columns of a table and can be assumed to hold a fixed number of values. The said values are all going to be the domain of the specific attribute.
- **Constraints:** Often ignored but highly important, constraints are basically fixed restrictions, rules and regulations which are followed to automatically assume different values as designated by the table

attribute. In our book, we are going to be following the standardized version which was revised quite recently.

Chapter Two: Concept Questions

Q1) What is a database?

a) A collection of information and records

b) A collection of binary numbers

c) A collection of specially selected files

d) A collection of media files

Answer: A

Q2) Which type of database is required to store the information of a number of multiple users?

a) Personal

b) Departmental

c) Enterprise

d) Professional

Answer: B

Q3) What is one of the main criteria of a good Database?

a) Not having a efficient storage system

b) Having a very complex filter system

c) Having a complex data retrieval system

d) Not having a way to prevent data lost

Answer: B

Q3) What are flat files?

a) A very complex collection of files of different formats

b) A simple collection of records of different formats

c) A very complex collection of information of a specific format

d) A very simple collection of data records in a specific format

Answer: D

Q4) When was the relation model first established?

a) 1990

b) 1980

c) 1970

d) 1960

Answer: D

Q5) What is a view?

a) A subset of a database which an application can use to eliminate all irrelevant data

b) A complete set of database which an application can use to use all of the data

c) A subset of a database which an application can use to add over existing data

d) A set of data which an application can use to add up more data

Answer: A

Chapter Three: The Different Components Of Your Database

By now you already know that SQL is a versatile language that is used to manipulate data in a Relational Database. Most Relational Databases to some extent use their own modified versions of SQL, but there exists an ISO standardized version as well, which is mostly followed to a great degree by developers and programmers around the world to manipulate data.

At first glance, SQL might seem like a relatively simple language. However, the versatility and depth of the language comes from the different components of the language itself. Each of them has their own specialty, giving the user a wide array of functionalities to play with and create their database. This in turn gives you the power to maintain, create, modify or even provide your relational database with a strong security.

- **DDL (The Data Definition Language)**
- **DML (The Data Manipulation Language)**
- **DCL (The Data Control Language)**

Throughout this chapter, we are going to be taking you through each of the sub-languages to a great depth.

DDL (The Data Definition Language)

This is essentially the component of SQL which fully allows you to define and create a database alongside its structure as well. Through DDL, you have full control over the very basic elements of the relational databases which includes views, tables, schemas and a whole lot of weirdly named things as well.

A Small Tip Before You Jump Into The Hype-Wagon

We are pretty sure that you must be feeling highly enthusiastic by now to start writing up your first entry into a database. But here's the thing: programming with SQL isn't like your traditional programming language where you should just blindly jump into the field and type in "Hello World". We are not saying you can't, we are just advising that you should not because that mostly ends up in disaster.

Building up a Database in SQL is more about planning out what you want to create beforehand, jot down everything on a piece of paper and create your blueprint first. The following points should help you while writing down the skeleton of your database, make sure to tick them off one by one:

- Make sure that you have properly identified each and every column and row, while defining the values which will be enclosed within those columns.
- Make sure to apply a unique key to your table. (Primary Key)
- Regardless of how many tables you make, keep in mind that you should keep at least one column common between them. This is required to ensure a logical link is formed between the tables.
- Make sure to put your tables in the 3NF or Third Normal Form in order to make sure that anomalies are not being inserted, updated or deleted.

Creating The Tables: The Fun Begins

So, we have already explained that a database table is very similar looking to a traditional two dimensional spreadsheet comprised of columns and rows.

The first command which you are going to use is "CREATE TABLE" to conjure up your table!

Once your table is up and running, then you will be able to start filling it up with data. Make sure to specify the names and data type of the columns beforehand though!

Linked functions of the DDL will allow you to further modify the stricter of the table using the "ALTER TABLE" command.

Alternatively, if you find that your table is of no use any more, then you may use "DROP" to delete it.

For creation however, you should keep in mind the command "CREATE" and "ALTER" to generate something new and change the structure respectively.

Let us show you an example now to make things clear. Suppose you are interested in creating a CUSTOMER table. Imagine now, what should be the attributes included?

Stuck? Let us help you then! You can include:

- CUSTOMER.CustomerID
- CUSTOMER.FirstName
- CUSTOMER.LastName
- CUSTOMER.City

And so on. The thing to note here is that the attribute that are created are closely related to the Customer. Naming conventions such as these will help you to organize your whole table with ease. Also a gentle reminder, most of the information stored in these field are going to be pretty much permanent!

Once you have specified the name of the column, you should then follow it up with type (INTEGER in this case) and constrain (NOT NULL for example).

Player	Year	Team	Game	At Bat	Hits	Runs	RBI	2B	3B	HR	Walk	Steals	Bat. Avg.
Roberts	1988	Padres	5	9	3	1	0	0	0	0	1	0	.333
Roberts	1989	Padres	117	329	99	81	25	15	8	3	49	21	.301
Roberts	1990	Padres	149	556	172	104	44	36	3	9	55	46	.309

Most of the application that you will use is going to give you some sort of a graphical interface that will give you something similar to the picture above.

Toying With The View

We have already discussed what the view command does. It simply helps you to filter out only the information which you need from specified columns and rows.

Keep in mind that the view has no physical substance and is just a virtual table, being a part of the database's metadata. However, the data which you are deriving from the created view are completely real.

Single Table View

The single table view is for those moment when you are going to need a data that exists only in a single table across your database.

The code looks like the following:

```
CREATE TABLE CUSTOMER (
CustomerID                      INTEGER
NOT NULL,
FirstName                         CHAR
(15),
LastName              CHAR (20)
NOT NULL,
Street                            CHAR
(25),
City                              CHAR
(20),
State                        CHAR (2),
Zipcode              CHAR (10),
Phone                     CHAR (13)
) ;
```

And below is the representation of the virtual table which you will create from the above code

Multi Table View

In most real life scenarios however, you are going to face situations where you will need to transact more than one data from multiple tables. Let's look at that problem by considering a hypothetical scenario where you work at a sporting goods store.

Say your current job is to let your esteemed customers know about your promotional offer. So in order for you to do that, you will need certain information from CUSTOMER, PRODUCT, INVOICE and INVOICE_LINE tables. To accomplish this task, you are going to create a multi table view to streamline the passage way of the data that you require. The following is the code for your program.

```
CREATE VIEW SKI_CUST1 AS
    SELECT FirstName,
           LastName,
           Street,
           City,
           State,
           Zipcode,
           InvoiceNumber
    FROM CUSTOMER JOIN INVOICE
    USING (CustomerID) ;
CREATE VIEW SKI_CUST2 AS
    SELECT FirstName,
           LastName,
           Street,
           City,
           State,
           Zipcode,
           ProductID
    FROM SKI_CUST1 JOIN INVOICE_LINE
```

```
      USING (InvoiceNumber) ;
CREATE VIEW SKI_CUST3 AS
     SELECT FirstName,
          LastName,
          Street,
          City,
          State,
          Zipcode,
          Category
     FROM SKI_CUST2 JOIN PRODUCT
     USING (ProductID) ;
CREATE VIEW SKI_CUST AS
     SELECT DISTINCT FirstName,
          LastName,
          Street,
          City,
          State,
          Zipcode
     FROM SKI_CUST3
     WHERE CATEGORY = 'Ski' ;
```

Let us dive a little bit further into the code now and dissect each of the itty bitty parts individually.

Below is the hypothetical database structure which you should be getting.

```
CREATE VIEW NH_CUST AS
        SELECT FirstName, LastName, Phone
        FROM CUSTOMER
        WHERE STATE = 'NH';
```

And as for the multi-view table, it should look something like this

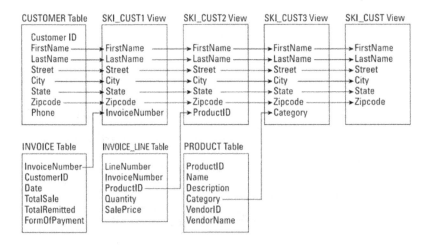

- The first statement integrates the columns of CUSTOMER table with a single column from the INVOICE table to generate the SKI_CUST1 view.
- The second line combines the SKI_CUST1 with yet another column from INVOICE_LINE table to conceive the SKI_CUST2 view.

- The third statement further adds up the SKI_CUST2 with another column from PRODUCT tables giving SKI_CUST3 view.
- Finally, the fourth statement helps to filter out the rows so it does not fall under the category of ski.

So, what are you finally getting? A view which is comprised of all the names and addresses of any customer who bought ski-related equipment for at least once!

Catalog And Schema

Schema is basically a separate organizational chart that is created using only the tables that are related to your requirements. But in some massive database system, even multiple schemas seem not to suffice in order to work efficiently. In situations such as these, SQL allows you add another layer of structure into the hierarchy which is named as catalog. Catalogs are essentially a big compilation of schemas, and the code for a catalog is as follows:

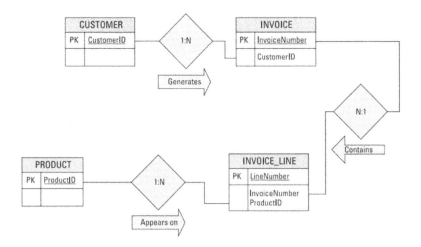

And with that, our topic of DDL pretty much comes to an end. We have included a diagram below to further clarify the different levels of hierarchy followed in a database structuring.

DML (Data Manipulation Language)

Following DDL, the next component that we would like to introduce you to is the Data Manipulation Language. While DDL's primary directives are to help you modify, create or destroy data structures, DML deals with the actual data itself. The set of commands that are used in DML are very similar to your everyday English and are easy to understand. But you should not let your guards down just yet though! The complexity of DML depends on the user himself and he can either keep things extremely simple or turn them into excessively difficult commands.

47

Some common expressions of DML with which you will be dealing include INSERT, UPDATE, DELETE, SELECT and MERGE.

Keeping that in mind, let us now look at some of the expressions with which you will be using throughout your journey.

Numeric Expressions

We have already mentioned earlier; Numeric expressions have everything to do with number manipulation. So, here you will be using the common mathematical operators such as addition (+), multiplication (*), Division (/) and of course subtraction (-)

```
12 — 7
15/3 - 4
6 * (8 + 2
```

But you are not necessarily limited to just numbers. The values can include host variables, column names as well as parameters.

```
SUBTOTAL + TAX + SHIPPING
6 * MILES/HOURS
:months/12
```

String Expressions

Strings tend to deal with a technically sentences, and here you will mostly be using the concatenation operator (||) which helps you to combine two individual strings into a one.

Expression	Result
'military ' || 'intelligence'	'military intelligence'
CITY|| ' ' ||STATE|| ' '||ZIP	A single string with city, state, and zip code, each separated by a single space.

Datetime and Interval Expressions

These expressions are used to manipulate the data of dates and times which falls under DATE, TIME, TIMESTAMP and INTERVAL. These expressions will give you the power to either add or subtract intervals from any given date time as well allowing you to specify your time zone.

An example would be

```
DueDate + INTERVAL '7' DAY
```

Another example where the program is designed to send a notice at the given time is as follows:

```
TIME '18:55:48' AT LOCAL
```

Alternatively, when you require an expression that deals with the due date rather than timing, you will have to use this:

```
DateReturned - DateDue) DAY
```

Boolean Expressions

These expressions simply check whether or not any given value is true and helps to direct the path of the program. Assuming that we have a program whose job is to retrieve information from a row titled "Senior"

The following code is going to retrieve the senior values

```
(Class = SENIOR) IS TRUE
```

While this one, is going to retrieve the records of all non-seniors ones

```
NOT (Class = SENIOR) IS TRUE
```

Predicates

The Predicates found in SQL are similar to various logical propositions. An example of a Predicate would be

"The student is a senior"

Assuming that we have table which contains information regarding various students, common domains of a CLASS column may include SENIOR, SOPHOMORE, FRESHMAN, JUNIOR or NULL.

Say that now you only want the row containing information regarding "Senior"

The easiest way to perform that is by using a predicate such as "CLASS = SENIOR" which will filter out all rows that would give a false value for SENIOR.

Logical Connectives

Logical connectives are very similar to predicate but different in the sense that these are much more flexible and allow you to create more complex predicates out of simple ones. So, say in a hypothetical scenario you are teacher of a high-school and you want to seek out child prodigies from your school. How are you going to do it? Well, it's easy enough! Bear in mind that the statements should read

" The student is senior"

" The student's age is less than 14 years"

And how are we going to create the code for this? By using the logical connective of "AND" of course!

```
Class = SENIOR AND Age < 14
```

Two more logical connective exists, namely OR and NOT. The difference between "AND" and "OR" is that in terms of AND, both of the predicates are required to be true. In OR however, just one requires to be true. The NOT logical connective on the other simply reverses the true value of any given predicate.

```
NOT (Class = SENIOR)
```

Set Function

Throughout your programming journey, it is inevitable that you may face situations where you are required to extract information not from just a single row, rather from multiple rows at once. To deal with situations such as these, SQL has a very organized set of functions, namely:

- COUNT
- SUM
- MAX
- MIN
- AVG

COUNT

This function allows to count the number of rows in any given table.

```
SELECT COUNT (*)
        FROM STUDENT
        WHERE Grade = 12 AND Age <14 ;
```

MAX

This one allows you to return the greatest value present in any given column.

```
SELECT    FirstName     , LastName
     , Age
     FROM STUDENT
     WHERE Age = (SELECT MAX(Age) FROM
STUDENT);
```

MIN

Similar to MAX, but this time it keeps an eye out for the smallest value in any given column.

```
SELECT    FirstName     , LastName
     , Age
     FROM STUDENT
     WHERE Age = (SELECT Min(Age) FROM
STUDENT);
```

SUM

This function is trivial in the sense that what it does is simply add up all the values in any given column.

```
SELECT SUM(TotalSale) FROM INVOICE;
```

AVG

As for the final one, this function will allow you to obtain an average value of all the specified values in a column

```
SELECT AVG(TotalSale) FROM INVOICE
```

DCL (Data Control Language)

The final component of the three is the Data Control Language system which comprised of basically four commands:

- COMMIT
- ROLLBACK
- GRANT
- REVOKE

These four commands are dedicated for protecting the database from any harm, either accidental or intentional (Hacking).

Understand The Protection Methodology

Now this is very important. You must understand that your database system is at its most vulnerable state when the system is about to perform tasks or transactions. Even if the whole procedure is confined within a single-user system, issuing a simple change might result in something catastrophic. A software or even a hardware failure might occur before the operation is successfully complete, leaving the database in a state of limbo.

SQL uses the above set of commands to make sure that only restricted operations are taking place during and only during verified transaction is being performed. The different steps which the system takes is as follows:

- If any anomalous action takes place before the transaction is complete, the COMMIT statement is run that ends the transaction.
- Alternatively, the ROLLBACK procedure is then used to scan the transaction log and carry out the process in reverse in order to return the system to its previous state.

The Mechanism Of User Privileges

It should be noted that the ability to cause harm to the whole database system in reality lies within the users. And as such, the designer of the schema (referred to as the owner) is given the options to set up a number of restrictions when designing the database in order to set the access privileges of different users. Some of the user are allowed to access only specific areas of the database freely. While other cases, the owner has the power to set up authentication tests to determine the allowance of users.

These operations are performed by using the protection commands of: seeing, adding, modifying, deleting, referencing and using.

A good programmer has the option to set up protection mechanism for most of the aspects of a database including:

- Tables
- Columns
- Views
- Domains
- Character Sets
- Collations
- Translation

Below is a table that wraps up all of the codes available in SQL which are dedicated to protecting the database.

To further clarify the case, let us give you a few more example. With the code below is enabling just a singular person, namely the sales manager to be able to see the customer table.

```
GRANT SELECT
      ON CUSTOMER
      TO SALES_MANAGER;
```

Chapter Three: Study Questions

Q1) Which one of the following is a SQL sub-language

a) DCL

b) DOL

c) DPL

d) DDL

Answer: D

Q2) Which of the following sub-language gives you full control over the basic elements of a relational database?

a) DDL

b) DML

c) DCL

d) DOL

Answer: A

Q3) Which point should be kept in mind while creating the skeleton of your database?

a) It is essential to identify each and every column and row properly

b) Never apply a primary key as it might make the database complex

c) Always make sure to put your tables in the 4NF form

d) It is always essential to keep at least two common columns between two tables.

Answer: A

Q4) Which command allows you to initialize a table?

a) INITIATE_TABLE

b) CRAFT_TABLE

c) GENERATE_TABLE

d) CREATE_TABLE

Answer: D

Q5) Which commands is used to change or alter the structure of a table?

a) MODIFY_TABLE

b) MODIFY TABLE

c) ALTER_TABLE

d) ALTER TABLE

Answer) D

Chapter Four: Learn To Build And Maintain Your First Database Structure Using SQL

You will always have the option to set up all of your database definition functions using simple RAD tools such as the integrated Microsoft Access tool. But since our book is going to help you master SQL, we are going to teach you how to achieve the same level of functionality and flexibility of building tables using SQL. Due to the lack of a streamlined graphical interface, SQL requires you to enter commands using your keyboard, while manipulating graphical objects might be a little tough on RAD, SQL on the other hand allows for easy manipulation of logical statements and strings.

Starting Off With SQL With The Help Of Microsoft Access

Understand this, that the Rapid Application Development tool or RAD for short is designed to be used with Access, requiring no knowledge of programing. It is possible to write and develop execute SQL statements using Access but it is essential to implement the back-door method.

The following steps are going to help you open a basic editor in Access to start writing your SQL codes

- Open up your database first and press the CREATE tab to bring forward the ribbon across the top of the window.
- Look for the Queries section and click Query Design.
- A dialog box should appear containing show table.
- Go ahead and click on the POWER table, after which close your dialog box.
- Next, click on the Home tab and press the View icon situated at the left corner of the Ribbon
- A dropdown menu will be available, showing the different kinds of view
- As expected, choose the SQL view to display the SQL view object tab and write down the following code.

```
SELECT
FROM POWER ;
```

After which, you will need to call upon the WHERE clause right after the FROM line while making sure to put an asterisk (*) in the blank area. A very common mistake which people make here is to forget putting the semicolon at the end of the line. Don't do that.

```
SELECT *
FROM POWER
        WHERE LastName = 'Marx' ;
```

- Once done, click on the floppy-diskette icon to save your statement.
- Enter a specified name and click ok.

Create You First Table

Before dwelling deeper into this, please keep in mind that even though we are teaching you how to create tables with Access, the information are not going to change even if you go for Microsoft SQL Server, IBM or even Oracle!

The only major difference is that in some cases you will be getting a visual guideline to help you, while in others you will have to adhere by the bland typing section.

So, let us have a look at the code for our first table then!

Since you have already opened up the SQL Access window, you are going to need to enter the following code in order to establish the foundation of your table.

```
CREATE            TABLE            POWERSQL
(
ProposalNumber       INTEGER
PRIMARY KEY,
     FirstName CHAR (15),
```

```
LastName CHAR (20),
Address CHAR (30),
City CHAR (25),
StateProvince CHAR (2),
PostalCode CHAR (10),
Country CHAR (30),
Phone CHAR (14),
HowKnown CHAR (30),
Proposal CHAR (50),
BusinessOrCharity CHAR (1) );
```

But at this point you might be a little confused as to where you should write this code right? Assuming that you are using Access 2013, just simply follow the steps below to initiate your POWER tool and start writing!

- First click on the "Create" tab on the Ribbon to allow display the icons related to creation
- Next, click on the Query Design icon
- Locate POWER and click on the "Add" button
- After that, press the close button
- Next, you will be needing to press the Home tab, followed by the View Icon situated at the left end of the Ribbon and choose SQL View

- Now, in the space where "SELECT From POWER" is written, wipe that text from the face of the earth and enter the code above.
- Once entered, press the red exclamation pointed Run Icon. Now your POWERSQL table should be created as shown below. Tada!!

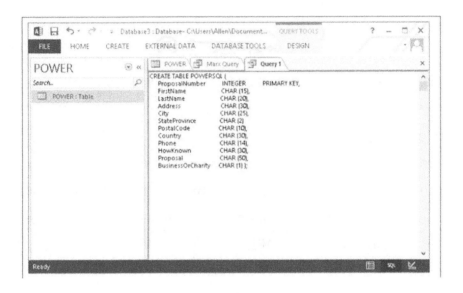

As we mentioned earlier, the information here is pretty much the same as what you would've entered through a graphical advantage. However, since SQL is a universally followed language, the syntax is transferrable to any ISO standard-compliant DBMS product.

Creating An Index

Once you are done with the basic structure of your table, the next thing you should learn is to create indexes. Now, these are very crucial to your database since they act as a kind of marker in your table to quickly help you pin point tables containing data of interest. These allow you to rapidly reach a specific point without needing to scan through the whole table.

But here's the catch. Unfortunately for God-unforeseen reasons, SQL doesn't internally provide a means to create these indexes. So, as an alternative method you will be required to use the built-in functionalities provided by the various DBMS vendors. Since these are not standardized, they vary from one vendor to the next. But you can safely assume that in most cases the commands are going to be similar, if not the same as CREATE INDEX.

Data Retrieval

Now that you are well versed in the ways of creating your basic data structure, let us sway ourselves a little bit more into how you are going to manipulate the data's in a Database.

Table Manipulation

Now that you have your table and index set up! You should know a little bit about how to alter the table once you have created it. Throughout your career, you will face situation where either by you or your client's decision, you will be required to alter the current state of the table. When that time arrive, a blank expression won't take you further throughout your career.

So, the very basics of altering the table structure will require you to enter the appropriate command indicating the alteration required.

The following code is when you will want to add a second address field in your POWERSQL table.

```
ALTER TABLE POWERSQL
    ADD COLUMN Address2 CHAR (30);
```

Again, when it comes to deleting a table, you will want to use the following code.

```
DROP TABLE POWERSQL;
```

Not as hard as it sounded before right? Bear with us and even the more advanced concepts are going to become much easier to you eventually! And amongst the various concepts, the most common one is the simple task which is retrieving the required information from a given database. Say for example, just the data of one row from a collection of thousands. The very basic code for this method is

```
SELECT column_list FROM table_name
     WHERE condition ;
```

As you can see, it utilizes the SELECT and WHERE statement to specify the desired column and condition.

Having familiarized yourself with the skeleton of the code, the following example should make things clear. Here, the code is asking for information from the customer.

```
SELECT FirstName, LastName, Phone FROM
CUSTOMER
     WHERE State = 'NH'
     AND Status = 'Active' ;
```

Specifically speaking, the above is an example where the statement returns the phone number of all active customers who are living in New Hampshire (NH). Keep in mind that the keyword AND is used which simply means that for a data to be valid for retrieval, both of the given conditions must be met.

View Creation From Tables

We have already discussed how the structure of a database helps to maximize the integrity of the data. You have to keep in mind here that within a normal database, there may be several applications who use the same data but might emphasize on specific data while working. The all-powerful "view" system of SQL will allow you to display and identify data that are structured differently.

The SELECT statement is what allows you to return the result in virtual table format.

In an example where the database is made up of CLIENT, TEST, ORDERS, EMPLOYEE and RESULTS. A view table can be conjured up using the SELECT command. Say that you want to create a view for a national marketing manage who wants to observe the state of the company's order. You are not going to be needing all of the information, instead you will be using just a few. The following code is how it should look like:

```
CREATE VIEW ORDERS_BY_STATE
        (ClientName, State,
OrderNumber)
    AS SELECT CLIENT.ClientName,
State, OrderNumber
    FROM CLIENT, ORDERS
    WHERE CLIENT.ClientName =
ORDERS.ClientName ;
```

Adding Data To Rows

Having created the shell your database, now you are going to want to add data right? It's simple. Just use the following syntax

```
INSERT INTO table_1 [(column_1,
column_2, ..., column_n)]
        VALUES (value_1, value_2, ...,
value_n) ;
```

Take note of the [] brackets. Any value you put inside these columns gets assigned to their respective columns accordingly.

Another example for a CUSTOMER table might look similar to

```
INSERT INTO CUSTOMER (CustomerID,
FirstName, LastName,
        Street, City, State, Zipcode,
Phone)
        VALUES (:vcustid, 'David',
'Taylor', '235 Loco Ave.',
        'El Pollo', 'CA', '92683', '(617)
555-1963') ;
```

68

Data Addition To Selected Column

Similar to the column, when you want to add data to a whole column instead of rows, you will have to utilize the following code

```
INSERT INTO CUSTOMER (CustomerID,
FirstName, LastName)
    VALUES (:vcustid, 'Tyson',
'Taylor') ;
```

Transferring Multiple Columns And Rows Amongst Various Tables

When you are working with larger databases containing multiple tables, Clients might sometimes ask you to create a completely new table or modify a table by filling it up with just a few information from different columns and rows from perhaps four other tables. These are scenarios where you will have to use the UNION relation operator to initiate this function.

Assuming that you have two tables, namely PROSPECT and CUSTOMER, in a scenario you might just want the list of the potential customers who live in Maine. The following is a code which you should be using

```
SELECT FirstName, LastName
    FROM PROSPECT
    WHERE State = 'ME'
UNION
SELECT FirstName, LastName
    FROM CUSTOMER
    WHERE State = 'ME' ;
```

Deleting Old Data

Nothing in this world is static and as time passes on, things are bound to become obsolete and useless. Same thing happens in case of data stored in database. At one point or the other, you are going to want to erase previous data to make way for new one or to simply clean up the whole database. For performing this action, you will need to use the SQL's DELETE statement which behaves in a similar way as the SELECT statement. The example below is going to remove the data of David Taylor from the CUSTOMER table.

```
DELETE FROM CUSTOMER
    WHERE FirstName = 'David' AND
LastName = 'Taylor'
```

Chapter Four: Study Questions

Q1) The RAD is designed to be used with what?

a) Access

b) Power point

c) Mozilla FireFox

d) Word

Answer: A

Q2) Which of the following can be used to data to a row?

a) INSERT UNTO table_1 [(column_1, column_2, ...,
column_n)]
   VALUES (value_1, value_2, ..., value_n) ;

b) ADD INTOtable_1 [(column_1, column_2, ...,
column_n)]
   VALUES (value_1, value_2, ..., value_n) ;

c) INSERT INTO table_1 [(column_1, column_2, ...,
column_n)]
   VALUES (value_1, value_2, ..., value_n) ;

d) ADD UNTO table_1 [(column_1, column_2, ...,
column_n)]
   VALUES (value_1, value_2, ..., value_n) ;

Answer: C

Q3) How can you transfer data between two tables, namely
PORSPECT and CUSTOMER

a) CHOOSE FirstName, LastName

    FROM PROSPECT

    WHERE State = 'ME'

UNION

SELECT FirstName, LastName

    FROM CUSTOMER

    WHERE State = 'ME' ;

b) SELECT FirstName, LastName

    FROM PROSPECT

    WHERE State = 'ME'

UNION

TRANSFER FirstName, LastName

    FROM CUSTOMER

    WHERE State = 'ME' ;

c) SELECT FirstName, LastName

    FROM PROSPECT

    WHERE State = 'ME'

UNION

INTO FirstName, LastName

    FROM CUSTOMER

    WHERE State = 'ME' ;

d) SELECT FirstName, LastName

    FROM PROSPECT

    WHERE State = 'ME'

UNION

SELECT FirstName, LastName

FROM CUSTOMER

WHERE State = 'ME' ;

Answer: D

Q4) How can you eliminate unwanted data?

a) ABOLISH FROM CUSTOMER

WHERE FirstName = 'David' AND LastName = 'Taylor';

b) ELIMINATE FROM CUSTOMER

WHERE FirstName = 'David' AND LastName = 'Taylor';

c) DELETE FROM CUSTOMER

WHERE FirstName = 'David' AND LastName = 'Taylor';

d) REMOVE FROM CUSTOMER

WHERE FirstName = 'David' AND LastName = 'Taylor';

Answer: C

Q5) How can you design a view with the following criteria – CLIENT, TEST, ORDERS, EMPLOYEE, RESULTS

a) GEENERATE VIEW ORDERS_BY_STATE

(ClientName, State, OrderNumber)

AS SELECT CLIENT.ClientName, State, OrderNumber

FROM CLIENT, ORDERS

WHERE CLIENT.ClientName =
ORDERS.ClientName:

b) INITIATE VIEW ORDERS_BY_STATE
(ClientName, State, OrderNumber)
AS SELECT CLIENT.ClientName, State,
OrderNumber
FROM CLIENT, ORDERS
WHERE CLIENT.ClientName =
ORDERS.ClientName:

c) DESIGN VIEW ORDERS_BY_STATE
(ClientName, State, OrderNumber)
AS SELECT CLIENT.ClientName, State,
OrderNumber
FROM CLIENT, ORDERS
WHERE CLIENT.ClientName =
ORDERS.ClientName:

d) CREATE VIEW ORDERS_BY_STATE
(ClientName, State, OrderNumber)
AS SELECT CLIENT.ClientName, State,
OrderNumber
FROM CLIENT, ORDERS
WHERE CLIENT.ClientName =
ORDERS.ClientName:

Answer: D

Chapter Five: Understand The Usage Of Advanced Operators

Based from what we have discussed so far, you should have a pretty clear idea by now that the whole structure of a database is very much interlinked with each other via the information distributed in various tables. Thus, the name 'Relational Database" comes into action. While most of the example used so far tends to work with information from just a single table, this chapter will focus mostly on the relational aspect and will teach you how to combine said information to provide a desired outcome.

The commands which we are going to be using in great depth here are the UNION, INTERSECTION and EXCEPT command alongside the most common ones from the family of JOIN operators.

UNION

The UNION operator in SQL is pretty much the same as its name implies. In the world of SQL, it behaves following the similar pattern as it did in the algebraic world. In a nutshell, the UNION operator allows you to bring up information from more than one tables which are made up of the same kind of structure and combines them together.

When talking about structure here, please note that we are referring to:

- All the tables must have the same number of columns
- The values in the corresponding columns should be comprised of identical data type and length

Let's say that you have two tables. One named AMERICAN and the other NATIONAL. Both are comprised of three columns with same type of data. The first table named NATIONAL holds the name of players and their statistics of completed games of only those who pitched in the National League. In case of the AMERICAN table, it's the same thing but that one holds the information of players who played in the American League.

Using the UNION command, you will be able to create a virtual result table which is made of all the rows from the first table and all the rows from the second table.

```
SELECT * FROM NATIONAL ;
FirstName        LastName
     CompleteGames

---------        --------              ----
---------
Sal             Maglie            11
Don          Newcombe         9
```

```
Sandy      Koufax        13
Don        Drysdale      12
SELECT * FROM AMERICAN ;
FirstName        LastName
     CompleteGames

---------      --------       ---------
----
Whitey     Ford              12
Don        Larson        10
Bob        Turley         8
Allie          Reynolds      14
SELECT * FROM NATIONAL
UNION
SELECT * FROM AMERICAN ;
FirstName  LastName
     CompleteGames

---------      --------       ---------
----
Allie          Reynolds      14
Bob        Turley         8
Don        Drysdale      12
Don        Larson        10
Don        Newcombe       9
Sal        Maglie        11
Sandy      Koufax        13
Whitey     Ford              12
```

One point we would like to mention here is the fact there is an alternative UNION command which is called UNION ALL. The difference between these two is that when using the first one, the duplicates will be erased. On the other hand, while using the latter one, everything will be joined up including the duplicates.

```
SELECT * FROM NATIONAL
UNION ALL
SELECT * FROM AMERICAN ;
```

INTERSECT

The action of INTERSECT is also similar to its algebraic counterpart. While the UNION command allowed you to combine all the elements of two tables, the INTERSECT command will allow you to combine only the columns that are common between the tables. The following example should make things clear.

The two tables which we are going to consider here are:

```
SELECT * FROM NATIONAL;
FirstName        LastName
CompleteGames

---------        --------        ---------

----
Sal        Maglie        11
```

```
Don          Newcombe          9

Sandy        Koufax            13

Don          Drysdale          12

Bob          Turley            8

SELECT * FROM AMERICAN;

FIRST_NAME       LAST_NAME

COMPLETE_GAMES

----------       ----------        ---

----------

Whitey           Ford                       12

Don              Larson            10

Bob              Turley            8

Allie              Reynolds         14
```

As you can see in the result, after the intersection has been made, we are only getting the information of Bob Turley.

```
SELECT *
     FROM NATIONAL
INTERSECT
SELECT *
     FROM AMERICAN;
FirstName        LastName
     CompleteGames
---------        --------          ----
---------
Bob              Turley            8
```

EXCEPT

While the UNION and INTERSECT commands mostly relied on two tables having similar information. The EXCEPT command works largely in the opposite direction, as it returns all the rows which only appear in the first table but lack from the second one. The syntax goes as follows:

```
SELECT *
    FROM OUT
EXCEPT CORRESPONDING (PhoneID)
SELECT *
    FROM PHONES;
```

The Family Of Join Operators

If you consider the UNION, INTERSECT and EXCEPT operators as Pawns in a chess game, then the families of Join operators are the soldiers of the higher echelon. While the aforementioned operators relied on multiple tables having something in common, the Join operators are extremely powerful operators who are able to join two or more tables regardless of the similarity (depending on the command of course). Whether source tables are comprised of a very low number of similar data, or even absolutely none! Join operators can still be used.

There are a number of Join operators in this family, but for convenience here we are going to be mentioning two of the most widely used ones.

The Basic Join

Any and every query which requires result to be enumerated from multiple tables can be considered as being a basic join. Specifically saying, the two tables SELECT with the exception of a WHERE clause is a perfect example of the most primitive type of join. We have already discussed about this in detail, but let us give you a more elaborate example now.

So, imagine here that you are a highly classified personnel manager of a large company and your foremost duty is to maintain employee records. Now in any large company, there are bound to be some information which is designed to be hidden from the public.

In this example, you will be creating such a table which only keeps the sensitive information aside and protects it with a password.

Assume that you are starting with these two tables:

```
        EMPLOYEE              COMPENSATION

        --------              ------------

        EmpID                 Employ

        FName                 Salary

        LName                 Bonus
```

City

Phone

And

EmpID	FName	LName	City
	Phone		
1	Whitey	Ford	
	Orange	555-1001	
2	Don	Larson	Newark
	555-3221		
3	Sal	Maglie	Nutley
	555-6905		
4	Bob	Turley	Passaic
	555-8908		

Employ	Salary	Bonus
1	33000	10000
2	18000	2000
3	24000	5000
4	22000	7000

Use the following query to create your virtual result

```
SELECT *
FROM EMPLOYEE, COMPENSATION ;
```

And the final output should look something like this

```
EmpID          FName              LName
    City       Phone      Employ
    Salary            Bonus
-----          -----          -----

    ----       -----      ------

    ------          -----
1          Whitey          Ford
    Orange     555-1001          1
    33000             10000
1       Whitey          Ford
    Orange   555-1001          2
    18000             2000
1        Whitey          Ford
    Orange   555-1001          3
24000             5000
1       Whitey          Ford
    Orange   555-1001          4
    22000             7000
2          Don          Larson
Newark 555-3221          1          33000
    10000
2          Don          Larson
Newark 555-3221          2          18000
    2000
```

2	Don	Larson		
Newark 555-3221			3	24000
5000				
2	Don	Larson		
Newark 555-3221			4	22000
7000				
3	Sal	Maglie		
Nutley	555-6905		1	
33000	10000			
3	Sal	Maglie		
Nutley 555-6905			2	
18000	2000			
3	Sal	Maglie		
Nutley 555-6905				3
24000	5000			
3	Sal	Maglie		
Nutley 555-690			4	
22000	7000			
4	Bob	Turley		
Passaic 555-8908			1	
33000	10000			
4	Bob	Turley		
Passaic 555-8908			2	
18000	2000			
4	Bob	Turley		
Passaic 555-8908			3	
24000	5000			

```
4            Bob        Turley
Passaic 555-8908        4          22000
        7000
```

Equi-Join

As we have already mentioned, the Basic Join comprises of the SELECT command without the usage of the WHERE clause. Equi-Joins are those where the "WHERE" clause filter is being implemented.

Let us have a look at the previous example so that you may observe the difference.

The code to be used here is:

```
SELECT *
      FROM EMPLOYEE, COMPENSATION
      WHERE EMPLOYEE.EmpID =
COMPENSATION.Employ ;
```

This should give the following result from the source tables mentioned above in the Basic Join section.

```
EmpID       FName      LName     City
Phone       Employ     Salary    Bonus
-----                  ------     -----
----    -----   ------    ------  -----
1           Whitey     Ford      Orange
555-1001 1          33000 10000
```

```
2          Don        Larson     Newark
555-3221 2            18000 2000
3          Sal        Maglie     Nutley
555-6905 3            24000 5000
4          Bob        Turley     Passaic
555-8908 4            22000 7000
```
Some Extra Details

While these are the most commonly known joins, there are some variants of these two which we have listed below for you to easily peruse through:

- **CROSS JOIN:** This is simply the command keyword for a basic join with the exception of a WHERE clause.
- **NATURAL JOIN:** This is considered to be a special case of Equi-join in which the WHERE clause has been used. The columns from the first and second table are compared and checked for equality.
- **Condition Join:** This one is similar in vain of an Equi-Join with the exception of the fact that the testing condition doesn't necessarily have to be an equality checker. It can instead be any properly defined predicate.

Chapter Five: Study Questions

Q1) Which one of the following is highly essential to use the UNION operator?
a) The tables must have different number of columns
b) The values of the corresponding table must all be of different lengths and type
c) All the table must have the same number of column
d) Few of the table must have the same number of column
Answer: C

Q2) What is the difference between INTERSECT and UNION commands?
a) UNION allows to only combine selected columns
b) INTERSECT allows you to combine all the elements in two individual tables
c) UNION allows you to combine only a single element from both of the table
d) INTERSECT allows you to combine only the column that are common between two tables
Answers: D

Q3) What is the specialty of the EXCEPT command?
a) It allows all the rows which only appear in the first table but lack from the second one to return

b) It allows only the first two rows which only appear in the first table but lack from the second one to return

c) It allows all the none of the rows which only appear in the first table but lack from the second one to return

d) It allows the last two rows which only appear in the first table but lack from the second one to return

Answer: A

Q4) Which one is the command keyword for a basic join with the exception of a WHERE clause?

a) NATURAL JOIN

b) Condition JOIN

c) CROSS JOIN

d) MULTI JOIN

Answer: C

Q5) A Condition join is similar to which join?

a) Equi-Join

b) Natural Join

c) Basic Join

d) Unconditional Join

Answer: A

Chapter Six: The Hard Hitting Concept Of Nested Queries And Recursive

Just as the title suggests, in this chapter we are going to be dealing with two very distinct yet crucial aspects of SQL programming. Let's start by talking about Subqueries first which will basically be covering the Nested Queries part.

What Exactly Are Nested Queries!

We have already discussed in details about the WHERE clause, Nested queries are basically the enclosing statements within the WHERE clause that defines what function the WHERE clause is going to perform.

NESTED Queries For Returning Multiple Rows

We will be elaborating this whole concept through the usage of a simple example. Let us consider for a moment that you are working for a world renowned company which specializes in assembling various components and bringing them together for you to conveniently purchase them. The whole structure of your company might be comprised of many tables, but you are only concerned with COMPONENT, PRODUCT and COMP_USED tables as illustrated below.

Product

Column	Type	Constraints
Model	CHAR (6)	PRIMARY KEY
ProdName	CHAR (35)	
ProdDesc	CHAR (31)	
ListPrice	NUMERIC (9,2)	

Component

Column	Type	Constraints
CompID	CHAR (6)	PRIMARY KEY
CompType	CHAR (10)	
CompDesc	CHAR (31)	

COMP_USED

Column	Type	Constraints
Model	CHAR (6)	FOREIGN KEY (for PRODUCT)
CompID	CHAR (6)	FOREIGN KEY (for COMPONENT)

The skeleton which you will be using here to acquire the information you desire is the formation of Subqueries with the usage of IN keyword.

```
SELECT column_list
    FROM table
    HERE expression IN (subquery) ;
```

The above syntax implies that the "WHERE" clause is going to be bringing out the information that is present inside the list to which the expression is pointing towards.

From the above example, if we want to bring out all the monitors from our company, we can write a code similar to:

```
SELECT Model
      FROM COMP_USED
      WHERE CompID IN
            (SELECT CompID
                  FROM COMPONENT
                  WHERE CompType =
'Monitor') ;
```

What this code will do is to return all the CompID for every present row where the CompType matches with "Monitor"

The opposite of the IN syntax is the NOT IN syntax which will bring out the information that does not contain the specified field. Following through our given example, if we wanted to bring out a list of all the products that did not fall under as MONITOR, the following code would've been used

```
SELECT Model
      FROM COMP_USED
      WHERE CompID NOT IN
            (SELECT CompID
```

```
                    FROM COMPONENT
                    WHERE CompType =
    'Monitor')) ;
```

Just as a head up, we would also like you to familiarize yourself with the DISTINCT keyword.

Using this keyword, you will be able to eliminate all the duplicate rows (if any) from your result with ease. The following example shows how that should be done:

```
    SELECT DISTINC Model
        FROM COMP_USED
        WHERE CompID NOT IN
            (SELECT CompID
                FROM COMPONENT
                WHERE CompType =
    'Monitor')) ;
```

Introducing The All, Any and Some Quantifiers

In the previous chapters, we have discussed a means of making Subqueries to return single values through the usage of comparison operators. Here, we are going to show you an alternative way which utilizes the above quantifiers.

Here you will need to use a combination of ALL, SOME or ANY quantifier with comparison operators in order to make sure that the final result is single value form.

Let us consider the table below:

```
SELECT * FROM NATIONAL
FirstName          LastName
    CompleteGames
---------          --------
        -------------
Sal                Maglie          11
Don                Newcombe         9
Sandy         Koufax          13
Don                Drysdale        12
Bob                Turley           8
SELECT * FROM AMERICAN
FirstName          LastName
    CompleteGames
---------          --------
        -------------
Whitey        Ford                  12
Don                Larson          10
Bob                Turley           8
Allie              Reynolds        14
```

Here we are going to making an assumption that we need all the information of pitchers who have completed the most game and are from American League. The code for the said example would be:

```
SELECT *
     FROM AMERICAN
     WHERE CompleteGames > ALL
          (SELECT CompleteGames FROM
NATIONAL) ;
```

This should bear the result similar to:

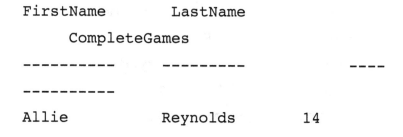

```
FirstName       LastName
     CompleteGames

----------      ---------              ----
----------
Allie           Reynolds      14
```

The Insertion Of Subqueries With UPDATE, INSERT and DELETE Statements

As you may already notice, subqueries are very versatile when it comes to being able to combine with different statements in order to manipulate multiple data. Combining the WHERE clause (with Subqueries) alongside any of the UPDATE, INSERT or DELETE statement you will also be able to obtain some pretty interesting results.

Continuing from the example of our hypothetical company, if at one point, we want to increase our credit for all last month purchases by 10%, would update our data as follows:

```
UPDATE TRANSMASTER
        SET NetAmount = NetAmount * 0.9
        WHERE SaleDate > (CurrentDate —
30) DAY AND CustID =
                (SELECT CustID
                        FROM CUSTOMER
                        WHERE Company = 'Olympic
Sales') ;
```

Dealing With The Concept Of Recursion

Now that we are done with the first part of this chapter, let us talk about Recursion. So, this is primarily a feature which has been around for quiet sometime in other languages. But it took an unfortunate delay to be integrated with the SQL framework. To understand recursion, you will need to understand a simple mechanism.

In any programming language such as LISP, Logo, C++ or SQL, whenever you are defining a function which will perform a specific action, the program automatically imitates that function by creating a command called "function call". A simplest example of recursion taking place would be a scenario where, alongside while performing a function, the function starts by calling itself!

To make things more clear, let us show you an example of recursion through a program written in C++ that has been designed to draw a spiral on your monitor. Keep in mind that it has been assumed that the drawing tool is initially pointing towards the top of the screen.

The code for the program is

```
void spiral(int segment)
{
        line(segment)
        left_turn(90)
        spiral(segment + 1)
} ;
```

When you are going to start the program by calling spiral (1) the following actions are going to take place

- Spiral(1) draws just a one unit line alongside the top of the screen
- Spiral(1) takes a 90 degree turn to the left
- Spiral(1) calls upon spiral(2)
- Spiral(2) draws just a one unit line alongside the top of the screen
- Spiral(2) takes a 90 degree turn to the left

And so on the cycle continues, until eventually you will end up with this.

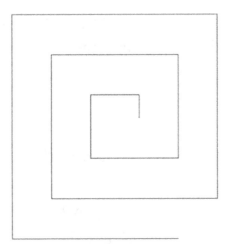

Notice how the program is calling upon itself over and over again? That is recursion. You can relate them to simple loops as found in Java.

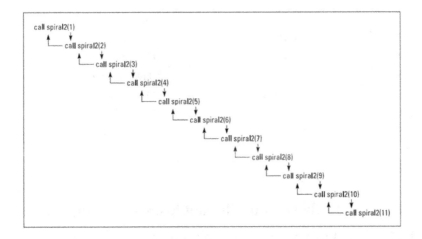

The Introduction To Recursive Query

Now that you know what recursion is, it should not be difficult for you to grasp the concept of a recursive query. This is simply a query which is functionally dependent upon itself. So, for example if we have an expression embodied within query 1, running that very expression would invoke itself in the body of the query expression.

Sounds weird? Don't worry! Let us clear things up with a real life example.

Let's consider in a scenario that a hypothetical Airlines called "The Secretive International" has decided to give you a completely free air travel opportunity. The obvious question that will pop up in your mind then is "Where can I go for free?" Below is a table which contains the flight number, source and destination of the available flights

Flight No.	Source	Destination
3141	Portland	Orange County
2173	Portland	Charlotte
623	Portland	Daytona Beach
5440	Orange County	Montgomery
221	Charlotte	Memphis
32	Memphis	Champaign
981	Montgomery	Memphis

Using the data above, you will want to create a complete table which will act as your vacation planner using the code below.

```
CREATE          TABLE          LIGHT (
    FlightNo        INTEGER          NOT
NULL,
    Source    CHAR (30),
    Destination CHAR (30) );
```

Once you have chosen a starting destination, you are going to want to decide which cities you will be able to reach. If say for example, you are starting from Portland or from Montgomery! Finding a solution to such a query can be outright cumbersome if you tackle each of the following queries one by one. This is a perfect example where recursive query should be utilized through the code below:

```
WITH RECURSIVE
    REACHABLEFROM (Source,
Destination)
        AS (SELECT Source,
Destination
            FROM FLIGHT
        UNION
        SELECT in.Source,
out.Destination
            FROM REACHABLEFROM in,
FLIGHT out
            WHERE in.Destination =
```

```
out.Source
            )
      SELECT * FROM REACHABLEFROM
      WHERE Source = 'Portland';
```

The result will be something similar to the table below which shows you through recursion, the possible reachable cities when starting from each of the source cities.

Source	Destination
Portland	Orange County
Portland	Charlotte
Portland	Daytona Beach
Orange County	Montgomery
Charlotte	Memphis
Memphis	Champaign
Montgomery	Memphis

Chapter Six: Study Questions

Q1) What is a Nested Query?

a) Enclosing statements within a WHERE clause which defines what the WHERE function is going to perform

b) Enclosing statements within a WHERE clause which defines what the JOIN function is going to perform

c) Enclosing statements within a EQUI JOIN clause which defines what the WHERE function is going to perform

d) Enclosing statements within a WHERE clause which defines what the WHERE function is going to perform

Answer: A

Q2) Which below syntax implies that the "WHERE" clause is going to be bringing out the information is present inside the list to which the expression is pointing towards.

a) UNDO *column_list*

   FROM *table*

   HERE expression IN (subquery) ;

b) CHOOSE *column_list*

   FROM *table*

   HERE expression IN (subquery) ;

c) SELECT *column_list*

   FROM *table*

   HERE expression IN (subquery) ;

d) MERGE *column_list*

    FROM *table*

    HERE expression IN (subquery) ;

Answer: C

Q3) What is the function of the DISTINCT keyword?

a) Will allow you to eliminate all duplicate rows

b) Wil allow you to pile up all duplicate rows

c) Will allow you to make multiple sets of duplicate rows

d) Will allow you to only a single set of the duplicate rows

Answer: A

Q4) What is the concept of recursion?

a) A process through which a function will prevent itself from launching

b) A process through which a function will run itself twice

c) A process through which a function will call itself once

d) A process through which a function will prevent other functions from calling

Answer: C

Chapter Seven: Making Your Database Secure

Being a system administrator for large scale databases is not easy as you may think. Not only are you going to deal with the demands of the clients, but you will also have to maintain and provide a much secured environment so that your clients can feel safe knowing that their data is in safe hands. SQL provides a diverse array of functions which can be combined to create very sophisticated and seamless security systems that will give you control over granting or revoking access rights to individual users.

The 9 Functions of Control

The following functions (all of which have been introduced throughout the prior chapters) contribute to the way you can re-enforce your security system.

- INSERT
- DELETE
- UPDATE
- SELECT
- REFRENCE
- USAGE

- UNDER
- TRIGGER
- EXECUTE

The Hierarchy Of Database System

When it comes to establishing a secured system, it is crucial that you understand the hierarchy of the database system. The hierarchy gives you an idea of how the whole system is working. At its very core, the parts of the SQL security system have been classified as follows:

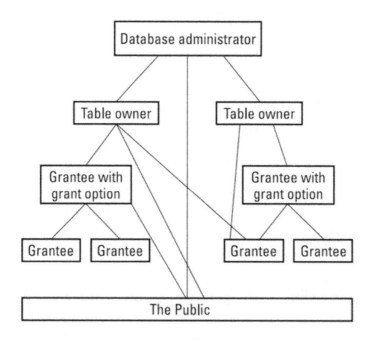

- **The DBA (Database Administrator):** The database administrator is generally the person who holds the supreme authority over all the actions occurring within a database. All the powers of modification are at the disposal of DBA and he can very well destroy everything with just a single mistake.

- **Database Object Owners:** This is another set of user with high privileges. In general, the people who create any data objects such as tables, views etc. are referred to as being the owners of those objects and they have privileges within them associated with the manipulations and protection of those objects.

- **The Public:** Once the DBA and Database Owners have been taken out, the remaining people working with the database with no special privilege are called the PUBLIC. The access rights of the public largely relies on the rights granted to them from the privileged users.

Setting The Privileges

As the DBA of a database, you will have the power to allow certain users access specific parts of your database and prevent them from accessing the rest. This is done using the GRANT statement.

```
GRANT privilege-list
     ON object
     TO user-list
     [WITH HIERARCHY OPTION]
```

```
[WITH GRANT OPTION]
[GRANTED BY grantor] ;
```

A Privilege here is defined as

```
SELECT
| DELETE
| INSERT [(column-name [, column-
name]...)]
| UPDATE [(column-name [, column-
name]...)]
| REFERENCES [(column-name [, column-
name]...)]
| USAGE
| UNDER
| TRIGGER
| EXECUTE
```

While an object is defined as

```
[ TABLE ] <table name>
| DOMAIN <domain name>
| COLLATION <collation name>
| CHARACTER SET <character set name>
| TRANSLATION <transliteration name>
| TYPE <schema-resolved user-defined
type name>
```

```
| SEQUENCE <sequence generator name>
| <specific routine designator>
And finally the user list is as follows
login-ID [, login-ID]...
| PUBLIC
```

The Significance Of Role Assignment

Roles are nothing but an alternative to user name which can be used as an authorization identifier. You can set a role using a syntax such as

```
CREATE ROLE SalesClerk ;
```

After which, you can assign people to the created role using GRANT

```
GRANT SalesClerk to Becky ;
```

This essentially will help you create a group of people with similar privileges with ease.

A role can be allowed to INSERT data by:

```
GRANT INSERT
     ON CUSTOMER
     TO SalesClerk ;
```

A role can be allowed to view the data:

```
GRANT SELECT
      ON PRODUCT
      TO PUBLIC ;
```

A role can be allowed to modify data by:

```
GRANT UPDATE
      ON BONUSRATE
      TO VPSales ;
```

Granting The Power To Grant Privileges

This concept somewhat works like granting other users whom you trust with a little bit of your power to control the database access privileges. This actually makes a lot of sense especially if you are attempting to work with a large group. You can't always be around, sometimes you may fall sick and at that point you are going to need someone to temporarily take over!

This can be done using the grant option, the below is the example of the sales manager that has been given the power to provide the UPDATE privilege to others.

```
GRANT UPDATE (BonusPct)
      ON BONUSRATE
```

```
TO SalesMgr
WITH GRANT OPTION ;


GRANT UPDATE (BonusPct)
    ON BONUSRATE
    TO AsstSalesMgr ;
```

Take Away Privileges

As painful as the title suggests, sometimes you might be required to take crucial and serious steps in order to revoke a user from his/her privileges. And this is done by the REVOKE statement as follows:

```
REVOKE [GRANT OPTION FOR] privilege-
list
    ON object
    FROM user-list [RESTRICT|CASCADE]
;
```

Understanding The Threats To Data Integrity

Now that you know how to control your structure, you should have a clear grasp of the most common threats which you might face that may hamper with your data stability.

- **Platform Instability:** Unexpected problems such as unseen bugs or problems in a new DBMS or operating system release falls under this category.

- **Equipment Failure:** This is, as the name implies, unforeseen events where your highly reliable state of the art equipment might fail sending your data to the afterlife. Keeping a redundancy backup which constantly copies everything will allow to protect against such an event.

- **The Problem Of Concurrent Access:** Even if you are completely sure that you program is free of bugs and hardware errors, problem might still arise if multiple users are trying to access your database at the same time. In situations like this the system struggles to decide who gets to enter first (Contention). A good method to tackle against this is to invoke a serialization system where the first user is given access first, then the second and so on...

Techniques To Reduce Possibility Of Data Corruption

While there are several steps that you can take in order to make sure that your data are safe. Here are some of the more common ones that you should be familiar with:

- **The Usage Of SQL Transaction:** This is one of the prime method through which SQL maintains the database integrity. We have already discussed about this earlier. It simply encapsulates all of the SQL statement which may affect the database and are only carried out using the COMMIT or ROLLBACK option.

```
Start of the application
      Various SQL statements (SQL
transaction-1)
   COMMIT or ROLLBACK
      Various SQL statements (SQL
transaction-2)
   COMMIT or ROLLBACK
      Various SQL statements (SQL
transaction-3)
   COMMIT or ROLLBACK
   End of the application
```

- **Isolation:** Another method is to isolate the individual transaction so that they are not conflicting with one another, even if multiple users are working at the same time. Using the SET TRANSACTION command, Isolation can very well lock up objects in the database if they are being fringed with in the wrong way.

```
SET TRANSACTION
      READ ONLY,
      ISOLATION LEVEL READ
UNCOMMITTED,
      DIAGNOSTICS SIZE 4 ;


SET TRANSACTION
      READ WRITE,
      ISOLATION LEVEL SERIALIZABLE,
      DIAGNOSTICS SIZE 8 ;
```

- **Usage Of Savepoints:** Combining the ROLLBACK and SAVEPOINT statements, the flow of a transaction can be controlled. The SAVEPOINT is set up essentially to terminate a transaction. This gives you the opportunity to roll back to the last save point should any problem occur right after the former transaction has been made.

```
SAVEPOINT savepoint_name ;
```
To Rollback
```
ROLLBACK TO SAVEPOINT
savepoint_name ;
```

Chapter Seven: Study Questions

Q1) Which of the following is not a function of control

a) INSERT

b) DELETE

c) SELECT

d) CHANGE

Answer: D

Q2) In the database system hierarchy, which of the following comes after "Database administrator"

a) Grantee with grant option

b) Table Owner

c) Grantee

d) The Public

Answer: B

Q3) Who holds the supreme authority over all the actions of a database?

a) Database Object Owners

b) Public

c) DBA

d) Database Modifiers

Answer: C

Q4) How can you take away privilege?

a) IGNORE [GRANT OPTION FOR] *privilege-list*

    ON object

    FROM user-list [RESTRICT|CASCADE] ;

b) DELETE [GRANT OPTION FOR] *privilege-list*

    ON object

    FROM user-list [RESTRICT|CASCADE] ;

c) REMOVE [GRANT OPTION FOR] *privilege-list*

    ON object

    FROM user-list [RESTRICT|CASCADE] ;

d) REVOKE [GRANT OPTION FOR] *privilege-list*

    ON object

    FROM user-list [RESTRICT|CASCADE] ;

Answer: D

Q5) Which one of the following is a threat to data integrity?

a) Equipment Failure

b) The Ease of concurrent accessing

c) Unstable Operating System

d) Both A and C

Answer: D

Chapter Eight: Understanding ODBC and XML Data Implementation

We have slowly ushered into a world where communication between machines and humans have become an integral part of any organization or company to maintain a satisfactory workflow. Sharing of information between and within companies across database networks plays a pivotal role in the grand scheme of the company's success.

However, the free sharing of information isn't as easy as it may sound. This is due to the different number of operating systems and applications available causing incompatibility issue. For this reason, the users especially the owners of large company have begun searching for an SQL extension tool that has the ability to allow freely sharing of information in between. This is exactly what ODBC (Open DataBase Convexity) system is!

How The ODBC Works

Given that both parties are using hardware that are ODBC compatible, a driver (in our case ODBC driver) is used to allow an application to access the shared database which has been carefully designed to be compatible with the database in question. The front end of the driver strictly follows the ODBC standard while the backend in most cases is customized according to the specifics of the addressed database.

The ODBC Interface

The ODBC Interface comprises of a set of definition that are required to establish a communication between the application and database.

- A Function-Call Library
- Standard SQL Syntax
- Standard SQL Data Types
- Standard Protocol for database engine connectivity
- Standard Error Codes

Breaking Down The ODBC Structure

The ODBC interface is technically comprised of four different components each of which plays an important role in making a transparent communication possible.

- The Application: The application is part of the ODBC which is within the user's reach. He/she uses the application to communicate with the database.
- Driver Manager: The driver manager is basically a DLL (Dynamic Link Library) provided by Microsoft for proper functioning of the system. The Driver Manager

loads up the necessary drivers for a system allowing the sources to transfer the functions to appropriate data via the designated drivers.

- Driver DLL: Since the source of the data can be different, a common medium is required to convert those data into ODBC compliant codes. The driver DLL is the component for this job!

- Data Source: The Data Source is just as the name implies. It is the source from which the data is obtained. It can be a Relational DBMS, A Indexed Sequential Access Method File or even a remote computer!

Introducing XML

The Various Data Types Of XML

Similar to SQL and any programming/ markup language, XML also has a number of different data types which acts as a user-defined type (UDT). Below is a list of the most common one's

- XML (DOCUMENT (UNTYPED))
- XML (DOCUMENT (ANY))
- XML (DOCUMENT (XMLSCEHMA))
- XML (CONTENT (UNTYPED))

- XML (CONTENT (ANY))
- XML (CONTENT (XMLSCEHMA))
- XML (SEQUENCE)

Scenarios To Use XML

Ultimately it will largely depend on the programmer whether he/she wants to implement XML into their SQL database. Here are some examples where the usage of XML is logical might include:

- When wanting to store a huge chunk of data
- When wanting to query a whole XML document
- When very strong data typing is required within the SQL statements
- To avoid incompatibility issues in the future
- To fully utilize the advantages of XML exclusive supports.

Have a look at the example below

```
CREATE          TABLE          CLIENT (
ClientName      CHAR (30)              NOT
NULL,
Address1             CHAR (30),
Address2        CHAR (30),
City                 CHAR (25),
```

```
State               CHAR (2),
PostalCode          CHAR (10),
Phone         CHAR (13),
Fax           CHAR (13),
ContactPerson CHAR (30),
Comments      XML(SEQUENCE) ) ;
```

The above table will be stored in an XML document in the Comments column of the Clients Table which will show something similar to the one below:

```
<Comments>
      <Comment>
            <CommentNo>1</CommentNo>
            <MessageText>Is VetLab
equipped to analyze penguin
                  blood?</MessageText>

            <ResponseRequested>Yes</ResponseRe
quested>
       </Comment>
        <Comment>
            <CommentNo>2</CommentNo>
            <MessageText>Thanks for the
fast turnaround on the
                  leopard seal sputum
sample.</MessageText>
```

```
        <ResponseRequested>No</ResponseReq
uested>
        </Comment>
</Comments>
```

Learning To Map SQL To XML

In order to exchange information between SQL database and XML documents, you have to understand how the database converts SQL elements into XML format.

Mapping Character Sets

Mapping character sets to XML is pretty straight forwards as you won't need to deal with a number of different character sets as in XML. The best method is to make sure that our XML characters are written under UNICODE and presto!

Identifier Mapping

Unlike SQL which is very lenient in terms of allowing you to use different characters as identifiers, XML is much strict. Allowed characters in SQL might be completely ignored by XML.

It should be noted that odd characters in XML such as $, % or & are allowed as long as they are kept inside double quotes. Another way is to convert the illegal SQL to XML identifiers to Unicode and then to hexadecimal code, to allow supreme problem free compatibility. For example, in XML an underscore might be represented by "_x00F_" or a colon might go by "_x003A_"

Integrating Your Data Values To XML

For converting data values, you will need to bear in mind that the SQL values should be converted to the closest possible XML Schema. For example, if you want to represent an SQL integer value in XML form, you will have to utilize XML facets such a maxInclusive and minInclusive to allow the values to be converted to the XML Schema.

```
<xsd:simpleType>
    <xsd:restriction
base="xsd:integer"/>
        <xsd:maxInclusive
value="2157483647"/>
        <xsd:minInclusive value="-
2157483648"/>
        <xsd:annotation>
            <sqlxml:sqltype
name="INTEGER"/>
        </xsd:annotation>
```

```
        </xsd:restriction>
    </xsd:simpleType>
```

Integrating Tables

Using the above methodology, you can also go ahead and map whole tables as well. It should be kept in mind that when the tables are being converted, they will keep their privileges intact.

```
<CUSTOMER>
    <row>
        <FirstName>Abe</FirstName>
        <LastName>Abelson</LastName>
        <City>Springfield</City>
        <AreaCode>714</AreaCode>
        <Telephone>555-
1111</Telephone>
    </row>
    <row>
        <FirstName>Bill</FirstName>
        <LastName>Bailey</LastName>
        <City>Decatur</City>
        <AreaCode>714</AreaCode>
        <Telephone>555-
2222</Telephone>
```

```
            </row>

    •

    •

    •

</CUSTOMER>
```

Creating The SQL Schema

Upon starting to map your data, you will notice that the first document which is generated usually contains the data while the second one holds the information for the Schema. Similar to Schemas for XML, here you will be able to generate is as such:

```
<xsd:schema>
        <xsd:simpleType
name="CHAR_15">
            <xsd:restriction
base="xsd:string">
                <xsd:length value =
"15"/>
            </xsd:restriction>
        </xsd:simpleType>
        <xsd:simpleType
name="CHAR_25">
            <xsd:restriction
base="xsd:string">
```

```
                    <xsd:length value =
"25"/>
          </xsd:restriction>
     </xsd:simpleType>
     <xsd:simpleType name="CHAR_3">
          <xsd:restriction
base="xsd:string">
               <xsd:length value =
"3"/>
          </xsd:restriction>
     </xsd:simpleType>
     <xsd:simpleType name="CHAR_8">
          <xsd:restriction
base="xsd:string">
               <xsd:length value =
"8"/>
          </xsd:restriction>
     </xsd:simpleType>
     <xsd:sequence>
          <xsd:element name="FirstName"
type="CHAR_15"/>
          <xsd:element name="LastName"
type="CHAR_25"/>
          <xsd:element
               name="City"
type="CHAR_25 nillable="true"/>
          <xsd:element
```

```
                name="AreaCode"
    type="CHAR_3" nillable="true"/>
            <xsd:element
                name="Telephone"
    type="CHAR_8" nillable="true"/>
            </xsd:sequence>
        </xsd:schema>
```

The SQL Functions That Are Operational With XML

There are some functions which SQL standard defines that when put forward towards a SQL database, conceives a XML results and vice versa. Below are the functions:

- **XMLDOCUMENT:** This operator is designed to take an XML value as input and return another value as output.
- **XMLELEMENT:** This helps to translate a relational value to XML compatible element.

```
    SELECT c.LastName
        XMLELEMENT ( NAME"City",
c.City ) AS "Result"
    FROM CUSTOMER c
    WHERE LastName="Abelson" ;
```

- **XMLFOREST:** This is responsible for creating lists of XML elements from given relational values.

```
SELECT c.LastName
       XMLFOREST (c.City,
               c.AreaCode,
               c.Telephone ) AS
"Result"
       FROM CUSTOMER c
       WHERE LastName="Abelson" OR
LastName="Bailey" ;
```

- **XMLCONCAT:** This also produces a list of elements by joining (concatenating) its XML formatted arguments.

```
SELECT c.LastName,
       XMLCONCAT(
               XMLELEMENT ( NAME"first",
c.FirstName,
               XMLELEMENT ( NAME"last",
c.LastName)
               ) AS "Result"
FROM CUSTOMER c ;
```

- **XMLAGG:** This is an aggregating function that takes fragments of XML documents as input and outputs them as one.

```
SELECT XMLELEMENT
    ( NAME"City",
        XMLATTRIBUTES ( c.City AS
"name" ) ,
        XMLAGG (XMLELEMENT (
NAME"last" c.LastName )
            )
    ) AS "CityList"
FROM CUSTOMER c
GROUP BY City ;
```

- **XMLCOMMENT:** This is a simple function that allows an application to create XML Comment.

```
XMLCOMMENT ( 'comment content'
    [RETURNING
        { CONTENT | SEQUENCE } ] )
```

- **XMLPARSE:** This one creates an XML value by doing a non-validating parse of string

```
XMLPARSE (DOCUMENT ' GREAT JOB!'
             PRESERVE WHITESPACE )
```

- **XMLP1:** This one allows an application to generate an XML processing set of instructions.

```
XMLPI NAME target
      [ , string-expression ]
      [RETURNING
             { CONTENT | SEQUENCE } ]
)
```

- **XMLQUERY:** This evaluates an XQuery expression and throws the result back to the SQL application.

```
XMLQUERY ( XQuery-expression
      [ PASSING { By REF | BY VALUE }
             argument-list ]
      RETURNING { CONTENT |
SEQUENCE }
      { BY REF | BY VALUE } )
```

The following commands are going to be used when dealing with Predicates that are specifically related to XML

- **CONTENT:** This can be used to check if an XML value is an instance of XML (ANY CONTENT) or XML (CONTENT)

```
XML-value IS [NOT]
     [ANY | UNTYPED] CONTENT
```

- **XML EXISTS:** This is used to determine if a value actually exists or not.

```
XMLEXISTS ( XQuery-expression
     [ argument-list ])
```

Mapping Array, Row and Multiset To XML

Rows

Assuming that we have an information field such as the one below:

```
CREATE          TABLE
CONTACTINFO (
     Name           CHARACTER (30)
     Phone          ROW (Home CHAR
(13), Work CHAR (13))
) ;
```

We will be able to convert it to XML following the below
Schema

```
<xsd:complexType Name='ROW.1'>
    <xsd:annotation>
        <xsd:appinfo>
            <sqlxml:sqltype
kind='ROW'>
                <sqlxml:field
name='Home'

        mappedType='CHAR_13'/>
                <sqlxml:field
name='Work'

        mappedType='CHAR_13'/>
            </sqlxml:sqltype>
        <xsd:appinfo>
    </xsd:annotation>
    <xsd:sequence>
        <xsd:element Name='Home'
nillable='true'

                Type='CHAR_13'/>
        <xsd:element Name='Work'
nillable='true'

                Type='CHAR_13'/>
```

```
                        </xsd:sequence>
        </xsd:complexType>
```

Which would generate

```
<Phone>
        <Home>(888)555-1111</Home>
        <Work>(888)555-1212</Work>
</Phone>
```

Array

For an Array, let's consider the following example:

```
CREATE      TABLE      CONTACTINFO (
        Name      CHARACTER (30),
        Phone      CHARACTER (13) ARRAY
    [4]
    ) ;
```

This can be mapped to XML following the code

```
<xsd:complexType
Name='ARRAY_4.CHAR_13'>
        <xsd:annotation>
            <xsd:appinfo>
                <sqlxml:sqltype
```

```
kind='ARRAY'

    maxElements='4'

    mappedElementType='CHAR_13'/>
        </xsd:appinfo>
    </xsd:annotation>
    <xsd:sequence>
        <xsd:element Name='element'
        minOccurs='0' maxOccurs='4'
        nillable='true'
type='CHAR_13'/>
    </xsd:sequence>
</xsd:complexType
>Giving the result

<Phone>
    <element>(888)555-1111</element>
    <element>xsi:nil='true'/>
    <element>(888)555-3434</element>
</Phone>
```

Multiset

The example phone numbers which we are using can as well
be mapped to a Multiset such as

```
CREATE            TABLE
    CONTACTINFO (
```

```
Name              CHARACTER (30),
Phone             CHARACTER (13) MULTISET
) ;
```

Which can be converted to the SML Schema:

Giving the result similar to

```
<xsd:complexType
Name='MULTISET.CHAR_13'>
        <xsd:annotation>
                <xsd:appinfo>
                        <sqlxml:sqltype
kind='MULTISET'

                mappedElementType='CHAR_13'/>
                </xsd:appinfo>
        </xsd:annotation>
        <xsd:sequence>
                <xsd:element Name='element'
                minOccurs='0'
maxOccurs='unbounded'
                nillable='true'
type='CHAR_13'/>
        </xsd:sequence>
</xsd:complexType>
```

And the result

```
<Phone>
     <element>(888)555-1111</element>
     <element>xsi:nil='true'/>
     <element>(888)555-3434</element>
</Phone>
```

Chapter Eight: Study Questions

Q1) What is required for ODBC to work properly?

a) Both party to have compatible ODBC hardware

b) Only one party to have ODBC compatible hardware

c) Only the front End to have ODBC compatible hardware

d) Only the back End to have ODBC compatible hardware

Answer: A

Q2) Which one of the following definition set will be required for establishing ODBC

a) Standard SQL Syntax

b) Standard Error Codes

c) A Function-Call Library

d) All of the above

Answer: D

Q3) Which component of the ODCB is basically the Dynamic Link Library of the infrastructure

a) Driver DLL

b) Data Source

c) Driver Manager

d) The Application

Answer: C

Q4) Which of the following is a perfect scenario for using XML

a) When you want to store small amount of data

b) When you want to query just a part of an XML document

c) When you want to avoid incompatibility issues in the future

d) When you want utilize just a part of the XML elusive supports.

Answer: C

Q5) Which of the following SQL Functions are operation with XML

a) XMLDOCUMENT

b) XMLDELETE

c) XMLREMOVE

d) XMLSELECT

Answer: A

Chapter Nine: Using A Cursor And Adding Procedural Capabilities

One of major problem faced by SQL programmers is the sense of incompatibility. Incompatibility may occur when SQL is coupled up with other applications. The difference comes from the fact that whenever you are trying to operate using SQL, it works on an entire set of table rows instead of just one. Luckily, we can avoid this problem through the use of a cursor. Cursor allows you to specify just a single table row using a pointer which then allows you to SELECT, UPDATE or DELETE the row.

Cursor Declaration

To actually set out on your quest of using the cursor, you must first conceive it by declaring it inside your DBMS using the DECLARE CURSOR statement.

```
DECLARE cursor-name [<cursor
sensitivity>]
    [<cursor scrollability>]
CURSOR [<cursor holdability>] [<cursor
returnability>]
```

```
FOR query expression
      [ORDER BY order-by expression]
      [FOR updatability expression] ;
```

Once declared, you will need to tackle some of the core characteristics of a cursor to further refine it to your preferences.

Cursor Sensitivity

The cursor sensitivity will allow you to control how many rows fall under your cursor's scope. It can be set through the code:

```
DECLARE C1 CURSOR FOR SELECT * FROM
EMPLOYEE
      ORDER BY Salary ;
DECLARE C2 CURSOR FOR SELECT * FROM
EMPLOYEE
      FOR UPDATE OF Salary ;
```

Scrollability

Scrollability is the determination of the capability of your cursor to be able to move around within a given set of results. This is achieved through the SCROLL keyword alongside the DECLARE CURSOR statement.

Bringing Your Cursor

Up until now we have only declared the cursor itself but haven't really brought it up into existence. To do that we are going to apply the code:

OPEN cursor-name ;

Specifically speaking, we are going to need to use the ORDER BY clause as follows:

```
DECLARE revenue CURSOR FOR
      SELECT Model, Units, Price,
                  Units * Price AS
ExtPrice
            FROM TRANSDETAIL
      ORDER BY Model, ExtPrice DESC ;
OPEN revenue ;
```

The Data Fetching Procedure

The data fetching procedure using a cursor is broken down into three steps:

- The first step is to declare the cursor with its name and scope
- The OPEN statement gathers up all the table rows that are selected using the DECLARE CURSOR query expression

- Finally, the FETCH statement is applied to actually get the data

The syntax for the FETCH statement is as follows

```
FETCH [[orientation] FROM] cursor-name
    INTO target-specification [,
target-specification]... ;
```

Keep in mind that here you will have 7 orientation options allowing you to work process your data accordingly

- NEXT
- PRIOR
- FIRST
- LAST
- ABSOLUTE
- RELATIVE
- <simple value specification>

Once you are done with your work, the final statement below will allow you to close down your cursor, assuming that you have followed the example which we gave here:

CLOSE revenue ;

Understanding How To Control The Flow

We are of course talking about the flow of your program here! As with many other programming languages, there exists some specific command statements in SQL that guide the direction of your program depending on various specified conditions. Using these helps to break the barrier of the non-procedural nature of SQL and allows to perform similar to a procedural language.

IF...THEN...ELSE...END IF statement

This is the most generic control statement in the computer verse and follows as one would expect The command is executed as long as the IF condition is true, the following statements are executed in opposite scenarios.

```
IF
        vfname = 'Joss'
THEN
        UPDATE students
            SET Fname = 'Joss'
            WHERE StudentID = 314159 ;
ELSE
        DELETE FROM students
            WHERE StudentID = 314159 ;
END IF
```

CASE...END CASE Statements

The CASE statement has been classified in two forms and the execution paths differ depending on which statement you are following.

The Simple CASE Statement

In this scenario, the CASE statement only evaluates a singular condition and then executes a following commanding by choosing from a number of branches.

```
CASE vmajor
     WHEN 'Computer Science'
     THEN INSERT INTO geeks (StudentID,
Fname, Lname)
          VALUES (:sid, :sfname,
:slname) ;
     WHEN 'Sports Medicine'
     THEN INSERT INTO jocks (StudentID,
Fname, Lname)
          VALUES (:sid, :sfname,
:slname) ;
     WHEN 'Philosophy'
     THEN INSERT INTO skeptics
(StudentID, Fname, Lname)
          VALUES (:sid, :sfname,
:slname) ;
```

```
        ELSE INSERT INTO undeclared
(StudentID, Fname, Lname)
        VALUES (:sid, :sfname,
:slname) ;
END CASE
```

The Searched CASE Statement

This is pretty similar to the Simple CASE, with the difference
of having multiple conditions to evaluate.

```
CASE
    WHEN vmajor
        IN ('Computer Science',
'Electrical Engineering')
        THEN INSERT INTO geeks
(StudentID, Fname, Lname)
            VALUES (:sid, :sfname,
:slname) ;
    WHEN vclub
        IN ('Amateur Radio',
'Rocket', 'Computer')
        THEN INSERT INTO geeks
(StudentID, Fname, Lname)
        VALUES (:sid, :sfname,
:slname) ;
    WHEN vmajor
        IN ('Sports Medicine',
```

```
'Physical Education')
            THEN INSERT into jocks
(StudentID, Fname, Lname)
     VALUES (:sid, :sfname, :slname) ;
     ELSE
            INSERT INTO skeptics
(StudentID, Fname, Lname)
               VALUES (:sid, :sfname,
:slname) ;
END CASE
```

LOOP...END LOOP Statement

The loop statement will allow you to execute then a similar sequence of statements repeatedly.

```
SET vcount = 0 ;
LOOP
     SET vcount = vcount + 1 ;
     INSERT INTO asteroid (AsteroidID)
            VALUES (vcount) ;
END LOOP
```

LEAVE

The LEAVE statement is pretty trivial and it works as expected. When this statement is established the embodying statement will be closed.

```
AsteroidPreload:
SET vcount = 0 ;
LOOP
     SET vcount = vcount + 1 ;
     IF vcount > 10000
          THEN
               LEAVE AsteroidPreload ;
     END IF ;
     INSERT INTO asteroid (AsteroidID)
          VALUES (vcount) ;
END LOOP AsteroidPreload
```

WHILE...DO...END...WHILE

The WHILE condition is similar to the loop condition, with the exception that a specific condition is needed to be met.

```
     :
SET vcount = 0 ;
WHILE
     vcount< 10000 DO
          SET vcount = vcount + 1 ;
          INSERT INTO asteroid
(AsteroidID)
               VALUES (vcount) ;
END WHILE AsteroidPreload2
```

REPEAT...UNTIL...END REPEAT Statement

This works similar to the WHILE statement with the difference that the condition is checked after the internal commands are executed after rather than before.

```
AsteroidPreload3:
SET vcount = 0 ;
REPEAT
     SET vcount = vcount + 1 ;
     INSERT INTO asteroid (AsteroidID)
          VALUES (vcount) ;
     UNTIL X = 10000
END REPEAT AsteroidPreload3
```

FOR...DO...END...FOR

The FOR Loop is used to automatically open and declare a cursor which will then fetch the rows falling under the cursor's scope and closes the cursor.

```
FOR vcount AS Curs1 CURSOR FOR
     SELECT AsteroidID FROM asteroid
DO
     UPDATE asteroid SET Description =
'stony iron'
```

```
            WHERE CURRENT OF Curs1 ;
  END FOR
```

ITERATE Statement

This statement allows the programmer to bring about a change of flow in the execution of any given iterated SQL statement. By iterated statement we are referring to the WHILE, REPEAT, FOR and LOOP statements.

```
    AsteroidPreload4:
    SET vcount = 0 ;
    WHILE
        vcount< 10000 DO
            SET vcount = vcount + 1 ;
            INSERT INTO asteroid
    (AsteroidID)
                VALUES (vcount) ;
            ITERATE AsteroidPreload4 ;
            SET vpreload = 'DONE' ;
    END WHILE AsteroidPreload4
```

Chapter Nine: Study Questions

Q1) Which of the following will allow you to declare a cursor?

a) INITIATE cursor-name [<cursor sensitivity>]

    [<cursor scrollability>]

  CURSOR [<cursor holdability>] [<cursor returnability>]

  FOR query expression

    [ORDER BY order-by expression]

    [FOR updatability expression] ;

b) OPEN cursor-name [<cursor sensitivity>]

    [<cursor scrollability>]

  CURSOR [<cursor holdability>] [<cursor returnability>]

  FOR query expression

    [ORDER BY order-by expression]

    [FOR updatability expression] ;

c) START cursor-name [<cursor sensitivity>]

    [<cursor scrollability>]

  CURSOR [<cursor holdability>] [<cursor returnability>]

  FOR query expression

    [ORDER BY order-by expression]

    [FOR updatability expression] ;

d) DECLARE cursor-name [<cursor sensitivity>]

    [<cursor scrollability>]

  CURSOR [<cursor holdability>] [<cursor returnability>]

  FOR query expression

[ORDER BY order-by expression]

[FOR updatability expression] ;

Answer: D

Q2) How will you be able to set cursos sensitity?

a) DECLARE C1 MOUSE FOR SELECT * FROM
   EMPLOYEE

   ORDER BY Salary ;

   DECLARE C2 CURSOR FOR SELECT * FROM
   EMPLOYEE

   FOR UPDATE OF Salary ;

b) DECLARE C1 CURSOR FOR SELECT * FROM
   EMPLOYEE

   ORDER BY Salary ;

   DECLARE C3 CURSOR FOR SELECT * FROM
   EMPLOYEE

   FOR UPDATE OF Salary ;

c) DECLARE C1 CURSOR FOR WHERE * FROM
   EMPLOYEE

   ORDER BY Salary ;

   DECLARE C2 CURSOR FOR SELECT * FROM
   EMPLOYEE

   FOR UPDATE OF Salary ;

d) DECLARE C1 CURSOR FOR SELECT * FROM
   EMPLOYEE

   ORDER BY Salary ;

DECLARE C2 CURSOR FOR SELECT * FROM EMPLOYEE

    FOR UPDATE OF Salary ;

Answer: D

Q4) Which one of the orientation option is available in the Data Fetching procedure?

a) NEXT

b) BACK

c) COINCIDENTAL

d) FINAL

Answer: A

Q5) Which of the following CASE statement has the ability to evaluate multiple conditions

a) Simple CASE

b) Searched CASE

c) End CASE

d) Start CASE

Answer: B

Chapter Ten: The Most Common Mistakes That Fools Make

Assuming That the Clients Fully Understand What They Require

This might come off as being rather a bit contradictory but let us lay down the fact here first. Generally speaking, any clients that reach out to you will ask you to design them a database that makes storing or retrieving of information they require a swift process. Now, you can simply follow all of the steps line by line but rest assured, the whole project will end up in a disaster. Why?

Unsurprisingly, most of the clients out there do not possess strong knowledge regarding this particular field in order to come up with the best solution possible. Following their guidelines might only put you under the red lights.

As an SQL Database Developer and Programmer, it is your job to always make sure that you are able to pull out the flaws from your client's initial design and convince them to re-enforce the whole structure accordingly. You make sure that, through your design, the final product meets up to their expectation.

Only Looking At the Project From A Technical Perspective

If you are newly budding and rising SQL developer, it is almost certain that you will be taking over your initial projects based on your technical prowess alone. This will show whether you are competent for that job or not solely relying on that factor.

However, we should warn you now that there a number of other factors which you should keep in mind as well. Such as-

- Budget
- Resource Availability
- Schedule Requirement
- Organizational Internal Politics

All of these could very well play a major factor in completely ruining a project however feasible it may seem and turn it into an utter nightmare.

Working Blindly without Taking the Client's Feedback

At this point, we are sure that one of two options scenario might swing by your head. In the first one, you might consider hearing everything which your manager has to say. Alternatively, there may be times when you would feel that listening to your managers is completely futile and effortless because they don't know anything about building up a proper database.

This is the point where we would like to intervene and warn you that you should never isolate yourself from the team. Doing so will guaranteed to push you towards darkness, so instead, try asking your managers the right question relating to the job at hand. It may surprise you to see how co-operative managers can be if you are able to lean them towards their comfort zone. Constantly bother your client and ask for their feedback to ensure that your whole project is going to the right direction.

Forcing Yourself To Work Only In Comfortable Development Environments

If you are an advanced programmer, then you have definitely honed your SQL development skills using a particular database which you now fancy a lot. But you should always keep in mind that every "application development software" has its own strengths which might make them suitable for one but not the other.

Not all of the projects that you will face are going to be in favor of your development environment and some might require you to stray from your current path. Whenever a situation like this might arrive, you should choose your next step very carefully. You could go ahead and face the challenge, cross over the learning curve and try to deliver something good. But there exists a very large risk of you not being able to deliver the promised product. On the other hand, you could let you client know that you are not up for the task and that they should hire someone else.

If abiding by strict professionalism, one should choose the latter option. But you are always open to go for the first one, just make sure that you are absolutely certain you will be able to cope up with all the hard work that might accompany you with that decision.

Making Up Your Mind That You Have To Design Database Tables In Isolation

When we are talking about Isolation here, we don't mean about locking yourself up in a room and writing the program all by you, no! We are specifically referring to the fact that you should not design a database table singularly without considering all of the other tables in your database.

The Database System as a whole is a very intricate and complex network of information. It sums itself up by taking quest from one table or the other before coming up with the final result. If you try to design a table by keeping it isolated from the others, chances are you will face complexities when you try to make that table work in conjunction with other tables in the database. As such, it is always wise to consider the whole network as a whole when designing your databases instead of tackling just a single one.

Avoiding The Beta Testing Phase

There is an old saying which implies that whatever works perfectly in theory, doesn't necessarily mean that it's destined to work in the real life. The same applies for large scale programs. The larger and more complex the program, the more possibility of it actually being drenched with a large number of bugs!

Now while your initial homebrewed is testing, you might think that since you are not facing anything, the program is good to go! But rest assured, once the program has been released in public, you are bound to be bombarded with a barrage of peculiar problems of which you probably never thought of!

This is exactly why Beta Testing is done. To prevent anything like this from ever happening! No matter how good of a programmer you are, you should always have your program tested out by a small group of people before handing over to your client to make sure that it is well suited up for real life scenarios.

Not Keeping A Thorough Record Of Your Whole Procedure

Throughout the whole journey of developing your program, once in a while you might start feeling too confident and proclaim that you will never need to touch the letters of your code ever again. For that reason, you figure you can stop documenting or keeping records of your progress.

Please be advised that such an act would do nothing but harm to you. Sure, right now you might be thinking that your program is immortal. But given the rate at which technological advancements are taking place, it won't take more than 6 months for your program to hit the hays, requiring you to update it once again.

Imagine yourself in such a scenario now. Without keeping any documentation, you won't even remember why you used that "WHERE" clause in the first place!

It's always better to stay prepared rather than face the troubles head on and suffer. As such, keeping records of your progress is highly important and should be turned into a good practice by every good developer.

Chapter Ten: Study Questions

Q1) Why is it important to understand the Client's requirements thoroughly?

Q2) Why is it really bad to just look at a project from a technical perspective?

Q3) Why is it important to take a Client's feedback?

Q4) Why should you try to come out from your comfort zone while interacting with a multitude of clients?

Q5) Why is it important to never miss the Beta testing phase of a project?

Conclusion

That has been a really long journey. I would like to take a moment of your time and thank you for purchasing my book.

The world of programming is literally comprised of a metaphorical entity that is constantly evolving and growing by adding new and new components. The SQL language which we have taught you here in this book followed the latest version at the time of writing, but maybe 3 or 4 years from now, this version might become obsolete!

But don't worry! The fundamental concepts are always going to be the same, there might just be a few new updates and additions here and there. And that is why after completing this book, we would advise you to keep on practicing and sharpening your skills until you become a master of database manipulation by not only taking quest from our book, but also from the well renowned websites such as W3Schools.com or Vertabelo Academy which only specializes in SQL.

By reading this book, you have unraveled the tip of the iceberg. Only through further exploration, you will be able to extend your knowledge and your potential to their absolute limits!

We wish you luck on your journey ahead and hope that you may become a successful icon in the world of SQL programming.

More On Our TechShelve

Python: The Ultimate Beginner's Guide For Becoming Fluent
In Python Programming
http://amzn.to/2e1MOKl

Contact Us

How can we make this book better for you?

Your suggestions, ideas, complaints will greatly help us. You can email us at Techshelve@gmail.com

Join Us -

You can receive offers and discounts on programming materials when you sign up for our email list: http://bit.ly/2cVwb18

www.ingramcontent.com/pod-product-compliance
Lightning Source LLC
Chambersburg PA
CBHW071200050326
40689CB00011B/2195